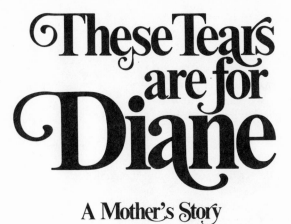

These Tears are for Diane

A Mother's Story

GOLDIE BRISTOL

WORD BOOKS
PUBLISHER
4800 WEST WACO DRIVE
WACO, TEXAS
76703

ISBN 0–8499–0020–4
Library of Congress catalog card number: 77–075468
Printed in the United States of America

Quotations from *The Living Bible, Paraphrased* (LB),
copyright © 1971, are used by permission of the publisher,
Tyndale House Publishers, Wheaton, Illinois.

The poem "Dead" by Martha Snell Nicholson is copyright
by Moody Press, Moody Bible Institute of Chicago, and is
used by permission.

The song "Wondrous Grace Hath Blest My Soul" by Muller and
Charles Weigle, is copyright 1943, renewal 1970 by John T.
Benson, Jr. International copyright secured. All rights
reserved. The quotation is used by permission of John T.
Benson Publishing Company, Nashville.

The song "Fill My Cup, Lord," by Richard Blanchard is
copyright 1959, Word Music, Inc., owner.

The picture on page 8 is by Craine, Detroit.

First Printing, February 1978
Second Printing, June 1978
Third Printing, August 1978

To my husband
Bob
and our two sons
Rollie *and* David
for this was a family affair

Contents

Foreword

This story was not written with the usual writing fluid; it is a heart-throb rather than a story. It brings before us the stuff of which life is made—joy, sorrow, despair, hope, pain, death —but also victory. Out of something that resembled the "blackness of gross darkness" came light and peace.

The "place" occupying the central place in this narrative is very beautiful. Let me describe it. In Michigan, along the eastern shore of Saginaw Bay there is a sandy strip of land jutting out into the not always friendly waters of Lake Huron. It is called, appropriately enough, Sand Point. It is four miles long and a half mile wide.

There is something delightfully strange about Sand Point. The community life of several small towns goes on around it; but, when the nose of the car turns from the main highway to the Sand Point road, one becomes aware that something has been left behind.

There is a quiet peacefulness surrounding the homes of those who obviously value sand, seclusion and sunsets. Stretching off to the north are the waters of Lake Huron. This is a picturesque setting for the cottagers. To the right one sees the sunrise, to the left the sunset, and straight ahead—the horizon.

Lake Huron has many faces, but whether it is the icy face of winter or the soft warm face of summer, the old lake seems too busy "doing its own thing" to bother about a strip of land called Sand Point. Many folks see the lake only during the friendly days of summer, but its winter face is fascinating. For several months, the shore is lined with huge unfriendly pieces of ice, something like teeth. They can almost snarl at the onlooker as if to say, "Don't you dare disturb our winter rest; if we are to put up with you during the summer, we need the rest of winter." Then, after awhile something happens—the "teeth" melt away, the winter frown vanishes, and strangely delightful is the sound of moving waters and the song of birds. The ground beneath one's feet seems almost alive.

The spring face of the lake is beautiful, and the beauty increases as summer takes over. Not all the cottagers on Sand Point appreciate the beauty; but, there are some with anointed eyes who can see God in all this. One of those was a girl named Diane Bristol. A casual snapshot shows her hair swirling in the wind, and her eyes fixed on the far horizon. Sand Point gave this unusual girl a few hours of sand, seclusion and sunsets. The picture seems to suggest that she was *listening* as well as *looking.* Maybe she was!

How much it cost Goldie Bristol to write this record we cannot know. It will cost you something to read it. Our prayer is that both the writing and the reading will be of eternal value.

SIDNEY E. COX

Introduction

After our daughter Diane died tragically at the age of twenty-one, a revolution began taking place in my life. Diane thought and lived as many young people are now doing. The last two years of her life presented a real challenge to my thinking. Since her death, I have been doing some honest, open looking at these thoughts. I have had to rethink, resort and review many important issues. Some fresh opinions have been reached regarding life and my faith, and I am profoundly grateful. Not only do I have Diane to thank, but my two sons and many of today's young people. I have been learning some valuable lessons in openness, honesty, tolerance and reaching out in love, as well as how to be flexible without compromise. I am still a student in the school of life and endeavoring to learn more every day.

My purpose in writing this book is twofold. One is to share Diane's life. The other is to share what God has been teaching me. At first, I thought of writing only in terms of its important therapeutic value. To release all these inner thoughts, to form them in writing, would keep me occupied for days and weeks. It would be good to keep reading, thinking, searching and praying as opposed to dwelling upon the very deep hurt in my heart. My attention would be focused on Christ and on learning what he had in all this for me. I knew this could become a growing experience if I allowed him to make it one.

The therapy aspect has been invaluable! But, could God possibly have further use for what had taken me weeks and months to write? Is there someone who might need to read the message on these pages? Could it be of definite value to others in any way? I have asked God to take it over and find a way to use it if he sees fit. I have left it with him.

God has proved many things to our family. We realize he has not eliminated darkness and pain just because we are his. We have had the wonderful opportunity, however, to experience his walking with us through the darkness. We have known the assurance of God's wonderful love and abiding presence. His strength makes it possible to face and to handle most anything.

My faith in God has been real for a long time, but now it has a new dimension. It has been made stronger and deeper than at any other time. This unique person, Jesus Christ, is at the inmost part of my being, and I desire to please him. This takes daily practice in the now, and my life is becoming rich and challenging. Each day is an adventure which God and I share together.

DEAD

Dead! So the sun cannot find her,
And the searching winds sweep o'er the plain,
And the peering stars lean from the heavens;
There are tears in the soft falling rain.

Dead! And the hearts that have loved her
Grow heavy with terror and dread
Of the years to be lived through without her—
The long, lonely years. She is dead.

Dead? Oh, then why that lark singing?
Our eyes are but blinded by tears;
Our senses are sodden with grieving;
The funeral dirge seals our dull ears.

Dead? When she roams Heaven's meadows,
Knee-deep in the daisies and grass,
With starry-eyed rapture of gladness
Which rose-tints the clouds as they pass?

Dead? She is breathless with wonder,
Understanding at last all His grace,
Just feasting her eyes on the Saviour,
On the loveliness of His face!

Dead? Can we call it dying—
That life that is filled to the brim?
Dead? In the light of His presence?
She is LIVING—forever—with Him!

MARTHA SNELL NICHOLSON

13

It happened Tuesday night, November 17, 1970. The following morning the San Diego Union *appeared with screaming headlines:*

**ATTACKED BY RAPIST—
GIRL'S BODY FOUND STRANGLED HERE.**

"The people that walked in darkness have seen a great light: they that dwell in the land of the shadow of death, upon them hath the light shined." Isaiah 9:2

1.
Cold Fear

November 18, 1970, seemed to be another quite busy day. We had expectations for enjoying the annual Harvest Banquet at our church that evening. I had taken time out during the morning to visit the hairdresser. On returning home, I busied myself with preparing pumpkin pies and sweet potatoes to take along to church. In fact, I was even planning on leaving early that afternoon to help with all those last minute hurry-up jobs. My husband, Bob, would come later with our special guest speaker, Dr. Sidney Cox.

My heart was singing a happy tune. The kitchen was filled with tantalizing aromas that accompany harvest dinners, and my appetite was increasing with each minute. It would be a very special evening, indeed, with delicious food, good fun, sweet fellowship and spiritual enrichment. We could always count on solid food for the soul from Dr. Cox.

I carefully placed the food I had prepared into the car, and it was time to leave. Just then the telephone began ringing. "Shall I answer it?" I thought. "If I had left one minute sooner I would never have heard it in the first place." One really can get hung-up on the phone. "Do I have time for that?" Better judgment told me it was always important to answer the phone.

I picked up the receiver and a strange voice said, "This is Western Union. We attempted delivering a telegram at your home earlier today but found no one there, so we will read it for you now over the phone. It is from the San Diego County Coronor: 'REGRET TO INFORM YOU OF DEATH OF DAUGHTER DIANE. PLEASE ADVISE AS TO DISPOSITION OF BODY.'"

Hot, then cold waves began sweeping over me—a most unusual sensation to describe. Had I heard right? This would never be the kind of thing for someone to be joking about. I asked to have the message repeated. Yes, I had heard correctly. It was truly information directed to the Bristols involving their daughter.

In a single instant the whole world around me went crumbling and my body became strangely numb. The church banquet which had seemed paramount was almost forgotten. I'm not really sure what happened to the food in my car. I did have presence of mind to call Bob immediately. His job with deadlines to meet and pressures to cope with could now wait. In fact, all the seemingly important things surrounding our lives that "must be accomplished" suddenly were not important at all. Our daughter . . . had died—and in an intensely terrifying manner.

When Bob got the details of Diane's death from the San Diego coroner's office, cold fear gripped my heart. Diane, twenty-one years old—gone—in a single moment. It couldn't be so! Only three weeks before, she had been home, radiant and active. All I could envision was her aliveness then as she moved in and out and about the house. Diane totally against violence, had met her death—and in such a violent way!

It seemed incredible, impossible, yet I knew it was so—terribly so—and in the knowing, such anguish overwhelmed me as I had not known. The tears came and they kept on coming until my head pounded with my furiously beating heart, and the whole world seemed wildly out of focus.

Yet in spite of reeling emotions, I was unquestionably aware of God's presence. Through the numbness and imbalance, I knew in my innermost heart that he knew what had taken place. My whole being reached up—way up—in that instant, only to discover he had already rushed down to meet my need. Underneath were his everlasting arms holding, sustaining and loving me. There was an assurance that through it all I would somehow hold together. I would not be cast adrift, but would be safe in his keeping.

I sensed also in that moment with God just how very much he loved Diane. He wanted me to understand this. With tears surging down my face, I cried, "O God, you have answered my prayer for Diane, I know you have—but I hadn't expected an answer so soon, nor in this shocking way."

We notified our two sons, Rollie and David. Within a few hours we were together in a state of unbelief. This kind of thing happened in *other* families, we knew. We had often read of this type of tragedy in the papers and had felt a certain amount of compassion in a general way. We had seen and heard news telecasts and had made the kind of comments everybody makes: "What is this world coming to? No one is safe on the streets anymore!" But *this* involved a member of *our* family. We realized, then, that we are never quite prepared to believe it could happen to us! But it had.

For the first time we understood as a family what it means to be completely shattered emotionally. Yet that shattering drew our little family close together. How fortunate we were to be a family, a family that cared.

> *"Yea, the darkness hideth not from thee, but the night shineth as the day: the darkness and the light are both alike to thee."*
>
> Psalm 139:12

2.
Diane

*D*iane was a greatly wanted child. We had two wonderful sons, Rollie and David. But to make our family complete, Bob and I believed that we should have a daughter. When the boys were nearly six and eight years old, Diane was born and our family completeness was realized. She was a healthy, lovely baby, and brought fun, joy and gladness into our home.

A few weeks after Diane's birth I wrote her a poem. I include it here simply to show our commitment of the children to God long ago.

> The good Lord gave you to us, Dear
> In answer to my plea.
> It seemed life would not be complete
> Without you, don't you see.
>
> I've thanked the Lord so many times
> For answering my prayer.
> I promised Him that if you came
> We'd gladly with Him share.

You've made us happy, baby dear,
And now you're in our keeping,
We need so much wisdom near,
And all the Savior's leading—

For we would teach you right, my dear,
Of God, and His dear Son
Who shed His blood on Calvary,
That your life should be won.

So—whether young or older, Dear,
Or far away may be,
To know that you belong to Him—
This is enough for me!

God honored that commitment, for by the time she was ten
Diane had given her life to Jesus Christ and received him as
her personal Savior from sin. As she grew older, our observation was that she sincerely loved God.

Diane always seemed to have a sparkle about her, and she
began singing very young. When she was only a toddler of
two, curly haired and chubby, I remember her being lifted up
on the grand piano in Sunday school. She sang clearly, completely uninhibited and in tune, "I am so glad that Jesus loves
me, Jesus loves even me."

One day when Diane was not much older, we were browsing
together in a Christian bookstore. She had wandered to the
next aisle and I could hear her humming and singing happily.
Suddenly a man's voice was speaking. I recognized it as belonging to a Baptist minister.

"Hello, little dumpling. I can hear your song. Tell me, do
you sing for Jesus in Sunday school?"

"Um-huh," came the reply.

"Will you sing one of your Sunday school songs for me,
please?"

Diane immediately obliged—with an uninhibited, "Make

mine Pfeiffers, Make mine Pfeiffers"—a television beer commercial!

Needless to say, I became even more absorbed with the books on the shelves in my aisle, and pretended for a while that I didn't know Diane.

I often imagined the minister thinking of that poor little child being brought up, possibly, in a godless home and perhaps even using the incident in his Sunday message as a classic illustration of the evil influence of television on the minds of children!

Diane moved from this cute toddler stage into the very awkward, self-conscious, plumpish, braces-are-beautiful years. She was a giggler too, like most girls that age. She often had friends stay overnight and the laughter went on until the wee hours of the morning. Then from all this she bloomed into full beauty and grace as a young adult, with a peaches-and-cream complexion and a disposition to match.

In high school Diane was a busy, happy girl, and joined all the clubs going. Warm and outgoing, she loved life and people, and they loved her. One of her music teachers remarked to me, "There is something about Diane that is always shining."

In her church life Diane was a member of a Dads and Daughters Quartet. I can still hear their song flowing forth, touching our hearts and lives at the last Christmas service before she left home:

> Beautiful Savior, King of Creation,
> . . . .
> Light of my Soul, my joy, my crown.

The last solo I recall Diane singing in church is one I can hear her singing now in God's presence:

> Wondrous grace hath blest my soul,
> I've been truly born anew;
> Grace hath saved and made me whole,
> Now I know God's word is true!

Diane was a greatly wanted child—
the girl to complete our family of two
boys. We enjoyed our family vacations
in the Michigan lake country. When
Diane was about 3 months old, we
spent it at Long Lake. As she grew
older, Diane learned to love the water.

Diane was a plump little toddler, and always seemed to have a sparkle about her. *Left:* Dave, Diane and Rollie posed for our Christmas greeting in 1952. *Below:* A year or two later the three of them sang for Christmas.

For a while Diane thought she wanted to own a horse. But her main interests were always musical. In elementary school she was part of a group, "The Musical Eight" (2nd from left, below left). Later she learned to play the guitar. Here she is singing with her brother Dave (below right). *Bottom:* The family together with Diane in her "braces-are-beautiful" stage.

Diane emerged into young adulthood with a peaches-and-cream complexion and a disposition to match. Warm and outgoing, she loved life and people and they loved her. *Starting top left, clockwise:* (1) Christmas 1966. (2) Graduation 1967. (3) Diane and Judy were college roommates. (4) On her 18th birthday we surprised her by inviting a group of friends over for dinner. (5) All dressed up for a formal date.

Oh my soul, praise thou Jehovah!
For this mystery divine;
Though I cannot comprehend it,
Yet I know this grace is mine.

This beautiful song of praise by Charles F. Weigle was used at Diane's funeral.

Diane enjoyed her Sunday school friends and all the functions of the church. For one Mother-Daughter banquet, she was asked to give the Toast to the Mothers. To my surprise and delight she honored the mothers with something she herself had written.

Search throughout the world
And take the most beautiful song
    a bird can sing—
And my mother's voice will sound
    much more sweetly.
Journey far and wide
And take the most beautiful flower
    you can find—
And my mother's face
    will be lovelier.
Stretch out
And feel the warmth of the sun—
I look into my mother's eyes
And see her smile—
    I feel much warmer.
Feel the cool rains
God sends down from heaven—
And the touch of my mother's hand
On my hot brow
    will feel cooler.
Look upon everything
That God created, in its place, perfect.
That is my mother
For God created her for me—
"Thank you, God."

Then she bent over to me and gave me a kiss.

Each summer Diane went to Youth Camp, and her counselor was always the "greatest." Being talented in drama, she would entertain the kids at camp with humorous readings. As I look through her Bible now and then, I find camp Bible study notes.

Her Bible has many underlinings and marginal notations. Some verses that are circled as well as underlined must have had special meaning for her. John 14:14 is one: "If ye shall ask anything in my name, I will do it." John 16:24 is another: "Hitherto have ye asked nothing in my name: ask, and ye shall receive, that your joy may be full." I wish I knew her thinking here.

One marginal note I especially appreciate; I find it reassuring that she understood Ephesians 5:30: "For we are members of his body, of his flesh, and of his bones." Her notation is, "We are as *safe* as Christ."

I cannot doubt that Diane knew Jesus Christ in a personal way. She was active in her Christian life. She was always enthusiastic about the Bible conferences and youth conventions. Each year she looked forward with great anticipation to College Day, and could hardly wait for the time when she would be a student at Grace Bible College in Grand Rapids. She took part in the church youth group with a real "want to" attitude.

Then, slowly at first, yet one by one, the questions began to be asked—the same questions that many others are asking.

During her last year of high school Diane began having doubts about herself and her faith. The sparkle and glow which had accompanied her from a little tot on was beginning to fade. She always seemed intent on seeking out a counselor's advice, and had many rap sessions with Miss Walsh, her senior high advisor. One afternoon she returned from school and wanted to talk with me: "Mom, I had a long talk with Miss Walsh today." A long pause. Was she trying to prepare me for something?

Finally I said, "Yes, hon, go on."

"She told me that if I continued in the direction I am now headed I will destroy myself." Another longer pause.

I looked at her intently, questioningly, lovingly, almost frantically—my mind racing wildly in many directions. Whatever does she mean? And for the first time in our very open and honest relationship, I knew I was afraid to hear the truth—whatever it was. Diane wasn't going to force me to listen, but I am certain she wanted me to know what was really going on in her life, and was giving me the opportunity to ask. But I didn't. Here is one point where I believe I failed Diane as her mother and friend. She needed my help, and in a sense was reaching for it, yet inwardly, I shrank from it. Consequently she didn't share what was on her mind that afternoon.

Now I ask myself, was she on drugs? I don't know. She didn't give any indication of it that we could see—but then we weren't expecting any such indications.

Diane became a troubled and unhappy girl. She no longer anticipated Bible College. I can only guess what she may have written on her application. She fully expected to be turned away and when the notification of her acceptance by the college came in the mail it took her by complete surprise. The dean told us later that when the board reviewed her application they decided, "Here is a girl who definitely does not want to attend our school, or else she is positively the most honest person in the world." Both reactions were right, I believe.

Since she had no other plans, we encouraged her to attend college for at least one year. "By then, perhaps you will know what you want to do with your life, and if so, we will not hinder you," her father promised.

All of Diane's doubts and fears and questions went to college with her, and they constantly plagued her. During the second term she became a dropout. At this point she said to us, "Please don't ask for any more singing from me. Right now I couldn't sing and truly mean it with my whole heart." This was a request that had to be respected. Too often we do things that we don't truly mean with the whole heart. Christ would

not have wanted it. (See Eph. 6:6.) I was glad for her frank-
ness and honesty.

Diane and I not only enjoyed our mother-daughter relationship but we were good friends also. We had many talks dis-
cussing things in life that were helpful to both of us—life's
values, a friend's confidences, the many loves of young people.
But just as Diane had lost her glow and her song, so we lost
our lovely relationship. The barrier was never so high that it
halted all communication, but a change had taken place. There
was a reserve and an aloofness not formerly present. She was
beginning to go her own way, have her private thoughts and
to share her confidences with someone other than her parents.

After she dropped out of college, Diane became a working
girl. She was saving her money to go to Hawaii. She had to
get away, live her own life, try her wings, do her own thing.
She expected that we would give her trouble, she said, but,
when Bob and I gave our permission, she was delighted, and
we were OK parents after all. We have never been sure our
decision was a right one. We believed, however, that she had
reached the place where she would have gone regardless of
our decision. She might as well go with our permission and
blessing, than to rebel and, as a result, lose all communication
between us.

Diane left for Hawaii on January 12, 1969. Two weeks
prior to that, Christmas Eve to be exact, she wrote a poem
which we came across after her death. It expresses some of her
true feelings, we believe, of how totally lost she sensed she
was and of her struggling and groping for God.

MY CRY

It's not always my loneliness that darkens the hour,
          but my unworthiness—
Not in meekness, but in pride I am brought down.
I have so far to go and there are so many walls to break.
With a straight eye I must go
          but from where I am standing

I can't even see the first step.

But I look back and see the steps already taken
    a great way I have come—
In my impatience I cry in desperation,
And that impatience is like an octopus with many tentacles
    squeezing out truth and hope and life—the light—
And I am drained and helpless and lost.

Oh wretched man that I am—
That much-heard cry is my cry also.
To God and all that is within me I plead
    for mercy and guidance
That I might be as He.

The day before we took Diane to the airport, we were in church together. Dr. Sidney Cox was guest speaker that Sunday morning. He was still somewhat a stranger to our family. His eighty-two years of life and many years of walking with God and studying his word meant that his life and message made an impact on all who were privileged to listen. After the service as people were dispersing, Diane slipped up to him and impulsively kissed him. He was surprised momentarily. Then placing his hands on her shoulders and with a look of "I understand" on his face, he said, "My dear, always remember that God's way is the best way." Diane's eyes filled with tears. I was observing this from a distance, and as I turned away I thought, "The right words spoken at just the right time." It was as though God had given Dr. Cox insight, and he understood the need and cry of her heart, when actually he didn't know Diane at all.

Diane's doubts and questions went to Hawaii with her where she stayed for six months. They then followed her to San Diego where she spent her last year.

Her very darkest moment was, we believe, in August of 1970 when she wrote to us from San Diego: would we please leave her alone. She was now twenty-one and could make it on her own. She would profit by her mistakes, "and I have made many," she confessed. She would untangle her own hang-ups, and would we please spend our time untangling ours. She would live her life in her way, she didn't need us. The letter hurt us, naturally. We hadn't been writing preachy letters— just casual notes, though we did say we were praying for her. But after talking it over, Bob and I decided we would respect her way and stay out of her life. It would be best for a while. We would let her make the first move.

Notwithstanding the darkness, I began to feel deep within a strange and unexplainable assurance that God had his hand on Diane. He was working in her life and was beginning to show me the answer to my prayer.

> *"I am the light of the world: he that follow-*
> *eth me shall not walk in darkness, but shall*
> *have the light of life."*   John 8:12

3.
Retreat

O God, you have answered my prayer for Diane, I know you have—but I hadn't expected an answer so soon, nor in this shocking way."

I have already referred to this prayer which welled up in me at the news of Diane's death. I want to share the background for it.

It was in the month of March, 1970, at Sand Point, the location of our summer home on Lake Huron. Dr Sidney Cox, who by now had become a personal friend, my mother and I had planned a spiritual retreat for three days. Dr. Cox refers to it as the "Sand Point Bible Conference," because he had brought with him a briefcase filled with taped messages by such men as Paul Rees, Alan Redpath, J. Sidlow Baxter, Stuart Briscoe, and others. Using the tape player we had two or three full sessions each day, listening to these men illuminate and clarify the Scriptures. We took notes, looked up Bible portions and discussed what we were hearing and learning, trying to assimilate as much as possible. It was a real spiritual feast.

One thing I enjoyed and looked forward to each morning following breakfast was our time of reading, sharing our thoughts on the Scripture, and then praying together. Dr. Cox is a genuine spiritual leader (he was eighty-three years old at the time), seasoned with the years, full of grace and wisdom. He had brought along a book by Roy Hession entitled *Be Filled Now*. I was delighted, for I had already read one of Hession's previous books, *The Calvary Road,* and was in the process of reading the second one, *We Would See Jesus.*

Roy Hession's books had challenged me to "right-now" living for Christ—being totally honest with God and with myself. I found that I had not been doing this, and wasn't even aware of this lack in my life. Now suddenly I was aware and wanted to do something about it. By confessing my sins and failures *now,* I can keep my relationship with God through Jesus Christ constantly fresh and up-to-date.

This was for me a fresh approach to the Christian life—a kind of continual revival within. I knew that any truth must wrap itself around one, grip the heart and become alive or it remains meaningless. The biblical truth contained in these books was suddenly grabbing onto my life and has brought about a real sense of freedom.

Roy Hession's third book, *Be Filled Now,* was new to me, and I listened eagerly as Dr. Cox read aloud two and three chapters at a time. We then discussed ways to infuse these truths into our daily lives so that they would become factual. Our sharing would come to a close with the uniting of our spirits in prayer. We asked God to make his Word come alive within us through his Holy Spirit, to enable us to live, not tomorrow, but now for Christ.

As a result of our Bible conference, every morning from that time on each of us comes to God and asks (1) to be cleansed from all sin through the precious blood of Christ, that we may be whole *for this day;* (2) that he would renew our minds so our thinking might be clear and Holy Spirit controlled *for this day;* (3) that the Holy Spirit of God would fill us completely *just for today.*

Some of my friends with whom I have shared this simple formula have adopted it for themselves and have excitedly reported their experiences of its workability. It seems a simpler way to live the Christian life—less encumbering—by placing each new day, with all that day will hold, back into the hands of our Father. After all, we *can* trust him for one day. Sometimes in looking at weeks and months ahead we forget to trust and are afraid, for it is too much to handle. But we can manage more easily on a day-to-day basis.

God does not change, we know, and our trust in him should be a sure thing. Being human (and our Father understands this), I find it easy to go right on being fearful and anxious. But as I practice trusting him for each new day, little by little my trust becomes stronger and more confident. Even though I often fail, I go right on practicing. If I have spoiled this moment, I need not be discouraged. My next moment need not be spoiled. By promptly presenting these miserable failures to God, I can rise above them and go on. I had become weary with mediocrity in myself as well as in others. I wanted to be alive in Christ today.

A fringe benefit of the Sand Point Bible Conference was the establishing of a regular Tuesday morning Bible study and prayer time at Dr. Cox's home. One Tuesday in May of 1970, Dr. Cox asked my mother and me if we had a particular prayer request. "I would like very special prayer for Diane," I told him. "I pray for her every single day, but I would request special prayer from this inner circle that God will bring Diane back to himself." Dr. Cox cautioned that we be sure of our motives. They must not be selfish ones. We must honestly want God in his way (not ours) to bring Diane back to a meaningful relationship with himself, and for his glory alone. We carefully examined our hearts, then together we deliberately presented Diane to God.

I experienced an unusual quiet assurance from God the Holy Spirit within my heart, and I knew God had heard our request. Afterwards, Dr. Cox said, "Now let us silently watch as God begins to work and answers our prayer in his way. And remember, he may answer in such a way as we're not thinking at all."

4.
Learning the Hard Way

*T*he family was together at Sand Point on Labor Day weekend, enjoying the last days of summer. The weather was most cooperative. We were having a wonderful time. There was just one sad note—Diane was not there to be part of this family weekend. She had just written us two weeks prior that we please leave her alone. Quietly, in my heart, I missed her.

Toward evening on Sunday, we were seated around the table, about to have dessert. We had commented on the fact that we still had Monday for vacationing, and were glad for it.

Then there was a knock on the door. To our utter amazement, there stood Diane, like a miracle out of the blue! Her arms were open, her face wreathed in smiles, and her eyes filled with tears. We had not seen her in over a year. She was looking wonderfully beautiful. Each of us wept for joy and sheer delight.

Again my heart quietly cried, "God, you are doing something for Diane. I don't understand it all, but I am beginning to see the answer to our prayer."

Was there an explanation? What could the answer be? A thousand questions pounded loudly in my head. What had brought about this decision? Why had she come home? Only two weeks before, she had asked us to please stay out of her life. Then Diane herself gave us the answer, "I felt compelled to come home. Something (or was it Someone?) seemed to say, 'Go home, Diane, without delay.' I was receiving good 'vibrations' from home and I knew the time had come to see my family again."

The impossible dream (or so it seemed) had come true. At long last Diane was home!

Not only did our family situation change, but even Sand Point became more beautiful. The sun presented a fantastic "spectacular" that evening as it set out over the waters of Lake Huron. It was as though God himself was surrounding us with heavenly light and love, actually entering into our celebration with us as we rejoiced together.

During the next two months we cleared our communication lines in open and frank talks. Diane was so open and honest it hurt, really. She made the comment, to our amusement, that her parents had "matured a great deal." She was probably right.

At this time we learned many things we would have otherwise never known. Diane had some very interesting, alarming and almost unbelievable stories to tell.

To begin with, before she made her trip to Hawaii, Bob and I had insisted she have a stated amount of money saved to take along. This would keep her going until she could find work. We also recommended a round-trip plane ticket as well, so she would be able to get home without difficulty should she run out of money. She complied with all these stipulations.

Diane had always been a very open and trusting person. She had not been in Hawaii even two weeks when some supposed friend conned her of all her money—plane ticket as well. She believed him when he persuasively said, "I have enough money in the bank to pay back all I am borrowing from you. Just meet me here in two days, at about eleven in the morning and I will have it all for you." But she never saw even a resemblance of him any time after that. He completely disappeared from her life.

"I was so angry at myself!" Diane told us. "How *could* I be that gullible? I really believed that all the now generation kids loved one another and could be trusted."

It was hard for her to accept the fact that some of those who cry and sing, "What the world needs now is love sweet love," would just as soon swindle. And now she was penniless and in a "far country" without a job. What was she to do? Her parents must not be asked to help. In fact, they must never know, for she had been determined to be independent and to make it on her own. Something would open up to her, it just *had* to. She admitted to extreme depression and discouragement.

But she also learned that people aren't all bad. There was the time she became desperately ill with a virus and a high temperature that got steadily worse. She was sitting in the park one day with her head resting against a tree, feeling too sick and weak to go on, thinking she would die. A young man whom she had never met approached her.

"You aren't feeling well, are you?" he queried.

Diane could hardly open her eyes but she managed to say, "That's putting it mildly. In fact, I'm very ill and I should see a doctor, but I don't have any money."

"Will you let me help you out?" he asked. "Obviously you can't go on like this. Come on, I'll take you to see a doctor."

After she had been checked by the physician and given a prescription, the young man paid the fee. He took her to the pharmacist, had the prescription filled, and then disappeared out of her life, just as completely as the swindler had. She never saw him again.

Diane recovered quickly with the proper medication and was deeply grateful to the young stranger. He was under no obligation to help, yet he showed compassion and kindness when she most needed it.

Diane told us how she spent her twentieth birthday in Hawaii. She had always been able to enjoy complete solitude and aloneness in the midst of surrounding beauty. Nature speaks and it has a message. She had chosen to spend the day on the mountainside overlooking the ocean. The sunshine was radiant. "I could almost reach high enough to touch the fluffy billowy clouds hanging low on the mountains. The sand and the sea sparkled and glistened. The sound of rolling surf was soothing—and I took time out to do some long and much needed thinking."

She had been away from home for five months, and had been learning many things of importance since then—but what *was* she going to do with her life? Was she honestly satisfied with the way things had been going? Had it brought about any kind of peace for her heart and mind?

What about God? He had been her whole way of life back home. She could not doubt him, she was surrounded with all kinds of evidence of his existence. Did he really love her personally? Was he directing her life because he was interested in her? How much guiding was she allowing him to do? Or did she have it "all together" fairly well with no need for him?

Diane knew her life was still empty. "Will I do anything about it?" she asked herself. She said, "It was a time for deep soul-searching. The whole experience was one I can't easily forget—the wind, the waves, the sun, the sand and God! The heights and depths, lights and shadows—the majesty of the mountains, the immensity of the sea, the vast openness of space, and the beautiful, beautiful quiet—and God!" But she did forget.

Then she met Brad. This was a turning point. Her attention was quickly and completely diverted from what God might want for her. Rather, an entirely new and fascinating interest became her focal point. Brad was a United States service man stationed in Honolulu. After dating a few times, they began to grow fond of one another. Eventually they decided they were meant for each other and belonged together. The life-style they adopted is characteristic of many of today's young couples.

They were happy, Diane told us, and Brad said he felt like a whole person for the first time in his entire life. He enjoyed music, and Diane tried to teach him to play the guitar. (We learned later that the scene in Honolulu was bad. They had become involved with drugs and things weren't good at all.)

When Brad was discharged from the service in July 1969, he and Diane flew to California, Brad's home state, where they made their home for the next year or so.

Diane had written a few very casual letters but had managed well to keep us in the dark about any specifics in her life. We did know that she was involved with Brad, but that is all we knew. I am sure God is wise in not allowing us parents to always know what is taking place in the lives of our children. When we learn of their experiences later, we shudder in fear and unbelief. Yet God had kept his hand on them all along. He had not forgotten to love and care for them. Being normal parents, we would have worried ourselves sick and possibly interfered. Diane already knew exactly what we believed and what our reactions would have been. Interfering would have been to no avail. It was best to leave her right in God's hands where we had placed her. He knew all about her life and in his love for her knew best how to deal with her. We did not. Yes, we prayed for her almost constantly and we were concerned, but we did try to "trust and not be afraid."

Diane also told us of her experiences (some of them) in California spent with Brad during the last year. It was not exactly all a bed of roses. She had a deep respect for Brad's mind. His unique thinking processes intrigued her, and she believed that all the arguments and answers he came up with must be correct. However, they were often foreign to anything she believed. He hammered away day after day, trying to convince her (and nearly succeeding) that she was not capable of using her own mind—she always accepted what she had been told and taught, never thinking anything through for herself. He made himself sound so logical and right.

She began losing all confidence in herself and in her ability to think rationally. Many hours were spent walking the shores of the ocean trying to sort out her thoughts. "Is what Brad is saying true? Is what he tells me right? Am I completely wrong? Is my faith in God really only that of my parents rather than of my own mind and heart?"

Brad even believed it was more important to straighten Diane's thought processes than find a job. First things first, after all! It was humiliating, and she felt belittled. "Well, I believe in working," she said, and so she did. She worked, earned the money and kept the bills paid. "Believing in the need for money is a false security," Brad would say.

Though his arguments sounded rational, Diane was becoming more and more frustrated and unhappy. Finally she had the good sense to seek the help of a psychiatrist. He strongly urged her to get away from Brad.

I don't mean to leave the impression there were never any good times. They went to concerts together and spent hours at home listening to music. There were times when they communicated well, which was something new for Brad, and helped him feel worthwhile.

They had some interesting adventures in eating and had some fairly sound thinking on nutrition. In spite of their lifestyle, they adopted the philosophy that anything which might be harmful to the body in any way should not be consumed. One evening Brad became violently ill after drinking an alcoholic beverage. The result was that he swore off drinking forever. In fact, they agreed together not to smoke, drink or use drugs. (So the drug hang-up was solved.) This also included the eating of certain foods and the eating of any food in excess. They were strong antipollutionists. They believed no one had a right to speak out on the subject if they themselves were polluting their own bodies. They had more on the ball in this area than many mature adults. It paid off well, also, for when we saw her, Diane's physical appearance was beautiful.

As Diane related these interesting and alarming incidents to Bob and me, not once did she really criticize Brad. If we said anything that sounded unfair in any way, she immediately sprang to his defense. "Mom and Dad," she said, "if you only realized his background you would understand a little better."

Brad was an only child born of parents older in years. He was also an only nephew and an only grandson. Therefore, being the complete center of much attention, he grew selfish and demanding, and usually got what he wanted. Diane left the impression that he wasn't loved much and was rather neglected. To her he insisted that there was no such thing as family love and ties. He experienced a great deal of misunderstanding in the family, and he did not relate to his father at all. He had no strong desires to remain home, and this was all right with his Dad.

"His people are indeed strange," Diane told us. "I never learned to know them too well. They were always nice to me, and we spent a Thanksgiving Day and a Christmas with them. But there were some necessary ingredients simply left out of Brad's life. I can't put my finger on the exact problem, but problem there was." Rather pensively she said, "My leaving him will just add to the lacks in his life, but it is something I just have to do."

Diane had come home to sort these things out, and that was the conclusion she had reached where Brad was concerned. She began to look and act and feel like her own self again, capable of doing some clear thinking and making decisions of her own—all on her own. She was regaining some of her self-confidence. At the same time her confidence in God was being strengthened, and the purpose of her life was coming into focus. She had been learning so many lessons in the past year and a half. In her own words, "I have been learning them all the hard way."

Recently Bob and I made a visit to Brad's home and have learned to know his mother. Her husband died some time after Diane's death, and because of these two experiences and the concern of a few friends, she was introduced to Jesus Christ and has received him as her Savior. I asked her about some of the impressions I had received from Brad and Diane about his home life, and told her that I truly wanted to be fair to her in my writing.

What they told me was probably just how they felt about it, she said, and I was not to change anything. "You were more successful with Diane than we were with Brad. At least Diane still wanted to go home. Brad did not." But that is changing now. Brad is more interested in his family and likes visiting his mother, and that has to be good. Whatever the home situation may have been, Brad's mother is now a fine Christian person and our sister in Christ, and we learned to love her.

*"Yet a little while is the light with you.
Walk while ye have the light, lest darkness
come upon you."* John 12:35

5.
Preparation

During the two months Diane was home, she visited almost everyone she knew, from her high school counselor to the girls with whom she had worked. She called on her friends, her college roommate, old neighbors, former teachers and still others. She felt compelled to do this, she said. It was as though she were getting everything in proper order for some unusual reason.

We watched with a tremendous amount of interest as God began to lift Diane from the depths of her frustrations and questionings into clearer thinking regarding herself and her Creator. The work had only begun, but something beautiful was unmistakably taking place within her heart and mind and life. She became intensely interested in her father's copy of J. B. Phillips's translation of the New Testament, and read for hours at a time. Bob and I prayed earnestly for the Holy Spirit to illumine each page and "open the eyes of her understanding" as she read.

Brad understood that one of Diane's purposes in coming home was so she might have all the time needed (from a distant vantage point) to carefully think through her relationship with him. She had doubts and many guilt feelings and believed she should break their relationship. She had said to us, "Oh, how I want to be right. If you only knew how much I *really* want to be right, but I have been so brainwashed I hardly know what is right anymore."

During the weeks she was home, Diane made entries in her journal. We came across them after her death. Here are a few which reveal a little of what was going on inside her.

Wednesday, October 7

My eyes and heart have been seeing good things since my last journal entry. For the past few weeks I've spent a "vacation" at home, here in the lovely city of Detroit and I've been glad that I have. (Lovely not used in its literal sense as I can't conceive of any city being actually lovely) but the *good* things that have happened to me here outweigh *that* factor. I soon will be ready to go back to San Diego because I do feel I must go back. I *think* I've become *really* aware for once of what I must do, and although it scares me, I have to do it. It scares me so much in fact that I fear to discuss it here at home until after I do it. Who knows, I may "chicken out," I feel stronger every day, though, that what I now feel is right.

Friday, October 9

I soon will have to say goodbye to every one. I shall miss them all again. It has really been good to see my friends and family. I found I am a lot closer to some of them than I had realized. But then, they have matured some and I have matured some and it is easier to communicate now. And my parents have gone through some good changes. I look at them (and they me) as individuals as well as parents and a mutual respect has grown. And I communicate much better now with my two brothers (I love them so much) and my sister-in-law. There is more love now in our family than there ever was. It's because we all realize *that* is more important than our differences. I didn't expect to find it so good—and I've also had a lot of time to do a lot of thinking.

Monday, October 12

The time to "face the truth" is drawing closer. I'm finding I'm quite afraid of that. I can't get over these terrible guilt feelings I have. Yet, if I make the right decision then I will feel better all the way around. I feel like I haven't even made it to the bottom rung of the ladder yet. It is too much to think any farther into the future than tomorrow. Tomorrow I can handle, next week I can't. I am trying to take one day at a time. I must exercise more faith, and what is right for me will work out. I believe that to be true. That is honestly my main desire—to do what is right in any situation.

Monday, October 19

I called my friend Kay today in California. She said she didn't know where Brad was living and he didn't want anyone to know. That gives me the feeling that he has intentions of finalizing our relationship too, which will make it much easier. Kay has most of my belongings and said I'm welcome to stay with her when I get back. That was really nice of her to offer. This will be a good week. I will be with good people, then spend some time at Sand Point and then I'll be kissing Detroit goodbye for some time.

Friday, October 23

I feel better every day. I am more sure of myself each day. I am not so afraid to face Brad anymore. I feel almost sure that he is happier living apart from me. I really needed to be away from him so that I could clearly see that it is wrong for me to stay with him. The past few days have been somewhat sad, but really good. I've been with the few people who I am closest to for the last time—or for a long time anyway. It is always sad to say goodbye to people one loves. But then, I never really leave them.

We were aware that Diane intended to return to San Diego. To sever her relationship with Brad, she felt it was necessary to talk with him face to face rather than by mail or telephone. Diane also told us that she really liked San Diego. "If I can

Our last pictures of Diane were taken at Sand Point in September and October 1970, just before she went back to California. They show "her hair swirling in the wind, her eyes fixed on the far horizon" (see p. 10). *Below:* Judy, Diane's college roommate, is on the left.

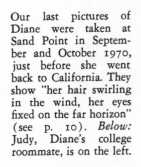

find a suitable place to work again, I'll probably rent an apartment and settle there. It's a beautiful place to live. I may even
reenroll in school and study music—voice in particular."

So, at the end of October when she announced she was ready
to go back, we were not surprised. We knew many important
issues had been faced and dealt with. Great strides had been
taken and God would continue the good work he had begun,
and work out his plan and purpose for her. It would have been
nice to have her stay at home, but she was of age and these
were her plans. We had already untied the apron strings, but
there were many other lovelier ties still intact.

On Monday, October 26, Diane boarded the plane for San
Diego. She had a new leather-bound copy of J. B. Phillips's
The New Testament in Modern English which she planned to
read while traveling—a gift from Dr. Cox. As she left us she
said, "Who knows, I might be back. If things don't go right
for me I'll probably be home before Christmas. I love you
both, Mom and Dad, and thanks for everything." She was
beaming as she waved goodbye. My eyes were misting but my
heart was happy. I could see that God was doing something
beautiful with her life, but I certainly didn't understand just
how beautiful!

We received one letter from Diane just three weeks after
her return to California. It was a cheerful letter. She had done
the important thing, the severing of her ties with Brad. Now
she was on her own. She had found work, a job that would do
until she found what she really wanted. "I believe my life is
pointed in the right direction at last," she wrote.

It looked as though Diane, at long last, was ready to begin
to live.

"As long as I am in the world, I am the light of the world." John 9:5

6.
Brad

A *woman living in a fairly comfortable and comparatively* safe residential area in San Diego was preparing to retire for the night. She turned out the light about 10:00 P.M. and went to lift the shade and open the window. Glancing out she thought she saw the form of a body lying in her driveway. Frightened, she immediately phoned the police. That is how our daughter's body was discovered.

When Bob called the investigators, we learned that Diane's death was of the most violent kind and had occurred sometime between 9:15 and 10:00 P.M. On the driveway beside her lay the literature and other materials she used on her job selling encyclopedias. People in the neighborhood confirmed that Diane was indeed on her job working. She had told us in her letter that working hours were from 3:00 to 10:00 P.M. Her employer was immediately contacted and he supported the fact that she was at work. He was to have picked her up at ten o'clock to take her back to the office, where she would then head for home. One person witnessed her crossing a lighted intersection alone at about 9:15 P.M. in the vicinity where she was found.

Although Diane did not consider selling encyclopedias a permanent job, she actually had sold two sets. The commission was good, so she was feeling quite excited. She had put some of this in her letter, and also on a tape which we received later with her belongings.

Ironically, we received Diane's letter in the mail the same day the telegram came with the news of her death. What a paradox it was, holding in one hand a letter in her alive handwriting telling us of present events, and at the same time receiving a telegram which shouted at us, "She's dead."

Diane's tragic murder naturally made the radio and television news in the San Diego area. When Brad heard it he was stunned. It couldn't have happened to her. It had to be a case of mistaken identity, he felt. Yet he knew that Diane had not returned to Kay's apartment. Distraught and bewildered, he did the only thing he knew to do. He phoned us. When our telephone rang and Bob answered Brad's call, the two men broke down and wept together.

"There is no one out here who understands," Brad said. "I'm facing this all alone. I'm torn apart, you know? Half of me is gone, what can I do?"

Bob tried to console him and explained as best he could that the only one who could really help him was God. "Turn to him, Brad," Bob pleaded.

A few hours later the phone rang again, and Brad was saying, "There's really nothing left to live for. Sure, we had broken our relationship, Diane and I, but I had every hope that in a year or two we'd be back together. I've been thinking it over and I've decided to commit suicide."

Our immediate reaction was, "Oh no, didn't we have enough weighing us down just now? O God, please don't let Brad kill himself!"

Bob tried to reason with him of the folly of such an act and attempted again to make him see how very much God cared about what he was experiencing. "He'll meet you, Brad, right where you are. He is so rich in the supply of everything you need just now. He wants so much to give it to you. Just reach out and believe him and trust him to do it." Bob then assured him that we were constantly praying, and that we understood what he was going through.

When the phone rang the third time, we began to fathom just how very real Brad's suffering was. He really had nowhere else to turn. He wanted to be talking with and feeling close to those he knew understood. "My relationship with Diane had made me feel like a complete person for the first time in my entire life," he told Bob. "There was a wholeness I had never known. I can't explain to you the torn-in-half feeling I'm experiencing."

"Brad," Bob said, "we wish you were right here with us. This is where you belong, for we love you. You are a very real part of what has taken place for all of us. I feel, in a sense, as though you are my son . . ." and he broke down and wept again.

As I sat listening, my own heart completely broken, I felt love reaching all the way across the country to Brad. We all needed one another. And then to hear Bob saying, "I feel, in a way, as though you are my son," I could hardly believe my ears. Only God could have put that kind of love in Bob's heart for Brad. After all, the kind of values he and Diane had taken on for themselves were not our kind! But Brad was a real person, one whom God loved and for whom Christ died. His feelings were genuine and he now needed us, and yes—we needed him. Only God could have made us feel this way.

Members of the family, and others, were sitting around the room taking in the scene. Finally, David hurried to the phone and said, "Dad, tell Brad we are wiring money for a round-trip plane flight to Detroit and back. Tell him to pull himself together and get things ready to come on the plane tomorrow." Brad hesitated at first—after all he didn't really know us, and he hardly believed in us. He wasn't sure he cared about funerals. Yet he knew he wanted to be with us more than anything else. He finally agreed to come.

Rollie, our oldest son, met Brad's plane the next day and brought him to us. Tall and slender, his dark hair and beard were long and windblown, his eyes filled with distrust and misgivings. We put our arms around him and sincerely let him know we were glad to have him with us. We wept together awhile, and little by little he relaxed and began accepting our love as genuine.

Now we were privileged to see this "son" of ours. His life did appear empty (through our eyes), confused and lost, as many of today's young people are. We were given this beautiful opportunity to show him acceptance and understanding, to share with him our love and mutual grief, and let him see Christ in our lives and in our home. What a tremendous responsibility!

Arrangements had been made to have Diane's body flown from San Diego to Detroit. All the necessary things that had to be taken care of we proceeded to do—the many phone calls and telegrams, the funeral arrangements, the visit with our pastor. But we were enriched and strengthened by the overwhelming response from so many friends. Every face, every card and letter, every flower had a message. Each one was seeking to express deep sorrow at a time when words are inadequate.

And then it was time for the funeral. Brad sat with the family during the service with no questions asked and no explanations given.

The message was given by Dr. Sidney Cox, our beloved pastor and friend. It seemed exactly right, just what Diane would have wanted. She was part of the "tell it like it is" crowd and would have wanted things basic and honest. In part Dr. Cox said:

I faced the perplexity of wondering, "What shall I say?" The difficulty was resolved when I remembered that the voice should be *her* voice, not mine. The message should be *her* message, not mine. It is not "What shall I say?" but rather, "What does she have to say to us?" As this will be, in some respects, her last message to us, it might be well to listen carefully. Her message will not be what she would have said to us one week ago, but what she has to say to us from her vantage point of *now*.

"First, do not presume to think that, and do not plan your future as if, you possessed an endless supply of the gift we call life. You may not have much of it left at all.

"Second, be sure to recognize that life is a gift from God, not merely the fact of life but the purpose of it and of the God who gave it. It was given to be used, not owned. We claim many liberties but the liberty to use life as we please is not one of them.

"Third, remind them that the most important fact of my life was and is that a personal relationship with God through Jesus Christ was established." I am quite sure she would say, "I was not always faithful"—have you always been? She probably would say that sometimes she was quite unfaithful—and how about you? The relationship she would have us remember now did not and does not depend on *her* faithfulness, but *his* faithfulness. It is not whether I hold on to God, but that *God holds on to me!* I can almost hear her voice saying, "Go right ahead, don't hesitate to say it—tell it like it is.

"Fourth, tell them for me, the young people especially, that God has already given us the answers to the problems we are vainly trying to solve. Tell them God has given us the answers in Christ—forgiveness for our personal sin, guidance for our personal pathway—hope for the future, strength for today.

"Fifth, remind them that God must have had an overruling purpose in all of this, and we must continue to pray that his purpose behind strange circumstances may be accomplished. Tell the folks to hold on to this.

"Sixth, tell them to hold on to the simple facts of the old faith. Jesus Christ is real and more wonderful than we had ever thought. There *is* a land that is fairer than day. Tell them it is true."

The overflowing crowd waited quietly in the presence of Almighty God as Dr. Cox asked us all to consider our relationship to Jesus Christ and respond to his love by receiving him

as our personal Savior or to renew our relationship by confessing our sin and experiencing his cleansing and forgiveness.
After the closing prayer, one young man, Gary, sought out
Dr. Cox and said, "I want you to know I did as you suggested,
and I've committed my life again to Jesus Christ."

With the funeral over, a great sense of relief swept over us.
We had done all we could. The days had been trying and
filled with strain, doing necessary things. The great flood-tide
of sympathy that had come rolling in, and had helped so
wonderfully, would recede. We would now have to make it
on our own.

Brad made preparations to fly back to California. His overall reactions regarding time spent at the funeral home and the
service itself, were hard to determine. He was very quiet and
uncommunicative with respect to it. David told us later that
Brad had indicated the whole affair was something he couldn't
relate to. He couldn't understand the "displaying of a dead
body," especially someone loved so much.

One comment Brad made pleased us very much: "I never
would have believed it if I hadn't come into your home to see
with my own eyes and feel with my whole being that this
thing called 'family love' is for real. Diane tried to tell me all
along that these kinds of family ties do exist, and I wouldn't
believe it. But I see it's true, for they are here and it's beautiful."

As Brad stepped on the plane, our hearts were longing after
him. "I'm going back to nothing," he had said on the way to
the airport. "I haven't known this kind of family love ever
before." We asked him to please keep Diane's new Phillips's
New Testament.

We keep on loving Brad and praying for him, hoping that
we will know the right things to do and say that will help
him open his heart and life to Christ and find out just how
much he is loved, how valuable he is to God.

> ". . . that ye should show forth the praises
> of him who hath called you out of darkness
> into his marvelous light."   1 Peter 2:9

7.
Coping

*H*ow do you cope when tragic situations come to a family?
Where does the strength come from? I've been asked questions
like these many times.

In the first place, as a family we had to ask ourselves where
this tragedy would lead us. Would we withdraw from the busy
world around us with our grief and sorrow? It would have been
easy to do just that.

But all the duties of life keep right on going, and demand
some kind of coping. Would we pick up all the loose ends
and dive into our activities to keep us from thinking? Thinking!
It just doesn't stop that suddenly, no matter which direction
one takes. Yet withdrawing to nurture our broken hearts could
have been disastrous. It certainly would have been physically,
mentally and spiritually harmful. Did we not have a God upon
whom we could continually cast every care? I knew that I,
personally, must now let him take over my anguish to use in
some unexplainable way to accomplish something beautiful
for himself. This was his concern, not mine, and I chose to
place my grief—and keep on placing it—into his all-wise hands
and trust him with it.

So I purposed not be absorbed with death, but rather with life—life in a new way; life that was fully alive; life to be lived openly and honestly. I found this is more easily said than done. But my aim is to live this kind of life every day. Tomorrow never comes—it is only my next now.

Bob and I also had to face ourselves honestly as parents. Our family has been a typical, average American family. Bob and I have had hopes, dreams and aspirations for success in our role as parents. We have had our moments of love and concern and growth together, and then our struggles and setbacks. We have experienced beautiful times of openness and understanding with our children. And we have known some extremely painful periods of withdrawal and little communication.

We have made many mistakes as parents. Some things we wish we could do all over again. It would be easy to harass ourselves for lacks of the past which cannot now be changed —"We've tried our best to be good parents. What did we do wrong? Where did we fail? We tried to set the example for right moral standards . . . what happened?" But we have determined to follow the biblical example. In Philippians 3:13-14 (LB), the Apostle Paul says, "I am still not all I should be but I am bringing all my energies to bear on this one thing: Forgetting the past and looking forward to what lies ahead, I strain to reach the end of the race and receive the prize for which God is calling us up to heaven because of what Christ Jesus did for us."

At the core of our thinking as parents was the desire to train our children in the Lord. We did this as best we understood. I'm sure we have insights now that were sadly lacking when we were young parents. God knows, however, that our greatest desire was to bring up our children in a way that pleased him.

Though we were remiss at times, we had family Bible reading and prayer, and tried to make them a part of our family life. I believe the children have been grateful for this. We experienced the joy of leading each one to the place where they received Christ into their lives. We were faithful in our Sunday school and church involvement.

Diane had a beautiful relationship with her two brothers, and looked up to them. I'm sure she shared special moments with them that we, her parents, were never privileged to know. They had a strong influence on her and she often turned to them for advice. I feel sure this influence rose up to meet her on many occasions when she was away and alone, attempting to do her own thing. I believe relationships are tools the Holy Spirit uses in his long-range strategy in preparing lives for God's purposes. We limited the Holy Spirit in our thinking when we forgot this. Our comprehension of his overall plan is so shallow and small.

What happens, then, in our children's minds that causes them to begin to doubt God and go their own way? I don't really know. Is it the work of Satan? It would be so easy to blame him, for he seems to be having almost unlimited influence on our young people. At the same time, we must remember that everyone has the freedom to choose. Our family is grown now, and each member must be responsible for his own life. What we have accomplished as parents is going to be seen in some measure in their lives, but we are no longer responsible for them. They must now answer to God for themselves as individuals. And our part is to trust them—their pasts and their futures—to God.

Finally, our ability to cope comes from God. God has not left us to find our way alone and to stumble in the darkness. He is that friend that sticks closer than a brother. Knowing that he walks the valley with us gives us the strength to cope. In his presence we derive freely all the things that really matter: grace, strength, love and, best of all, his constant abiding. He never leaves us for a single moment. Rays of light do filter through the dark clouds as we walk with him. Even in the tears and darkness, the light of Christ's presence breaks through in rainbow colors.

Several people told us that in the time at the funeral home they saw a quiet beauty in our family. Beauty in death? Our hearts were crushed. Certainly Diane's death was not a thing of beauty. The boys had lost a loved sister. Bob had lost his daughter, the "apple of his eye." He had said, "O God, I would have gladly died in her place—she was so young, so alive and ready to live." I had lost the one closest to a mother's heart and could only feel pain and hurt. Yet all those dear friends who had come to share our grief could see beauty? It was difficult to understand.

David said, "Mom, different guests have spoken of your radiant faith and strength. They came here to console you, but instead are being lifted up and fortified themselves by what they are observing."

Radiance? Beauty? Faith? Strength? We were unaware of any of it. We were simply a broken-hearted family who had faith in God and, unbeknownst to us, the beauty was there. It was not our beauty or serenity at all. It had to be Christ using the shattering circumstances of our lives to unveil himself. We could not have accomplished this if we had tried for a hundred years. The experience is difficult to explain. It just happens when we drop everything into the lap of God and allow him to take complete charge. Then there is coping, there is strength, there is something beautiful!

"The desert shall rejoice, and blossom as the rose. It shall blossom abundantly, and rejoice even with joy and singing. . . . in the wilderness shall the waters break out, and streams in the desert. And the ransomed of the Lord shall return . . . to Zion with songs and everlasting joy upon their heads: they shall obtain joy and gladness, and sorrow and sighing shall flee away" (Isa. 35:1, 2, 6, 10).

*"I am come a light into the world, that who-
soever believeth on me should not abide in
darkness."* John 12:46

8
Hindsight

*N*one of us can see into the future and be prepared for the
hard knocks of life which come our way. But the pattern of
the past few years makes me believe that God is constantly
preparing us for crisis. Until I started writing this book, I hadn't
thought about that before. God is intensely interested in me
this very minute and loves me without any kind of interrup-
tion. He has my best interests at heart, and is concerned about
what happens in the deepest places of my life. So why wouldn't
his preparations for my future be an ongoing thing, nonstop?
Even though he keeps the future veiled, he is steadily strength-
ening and firming up my spiritual and emotional muscles so I
am ready (to a degree at least) for what he knows is coming.

Many events of the past few years would have gone unrecog-
nized as God-planned had our crisis not come. It often takes
hindsight to understand God's provisions. He is always reaching our way, undergirding at the exact moment it is needed.
According to Psalm 139, he does not take his mind off us for
one minute. As one friend of ours has said (referring to Psalm
121:4), "We are kept by the insomnia of God, an unsleeping
love." Let me share a few experiences to help make this clear.

To begin with, God most certainly did the arranging when Dr. Sidney Cox was brought into our lives. It was no accident that he was available to become the temporary pastor of our church. Bob and I got to know him personally because we were privileged to give him transportation. His Spirit-filled ministry and his unique presentation of the Word of God fascinated us. He was one of God's giants, and we were richer for knowing him. He soon became part of the family, and we loved him as our own father. God knew that the wisdom and counsel he gave us from the pulpit and in person during those months before Diane's death would be really needed. It was as though the cupboards of our souls were storing up meat and drink for a time when physical food would lose all appeal. God knew this man would be a tower of strength when we desperately needed such a tower. God makes no mistakes, and Dr. Cox was ushered into our lives in an intimate way at precisely God's timing.

I believe the "Sand Point Bible Conference" of March 1970, was another of God's steps in fitting me for impending suffering. I've already referred to the spiritual enrichment I received leading to a renewed and refreshing relationship with God through his Holy Spirit. Through coming to God every day for cleansing and placing back into his keeping all that each day holds, including myself, I had experienced growth—had put down roots into Christ and my faith had become increasingly strong. Looking back on the conference experience now, I see it happening for a definite purpose. When the impact of unexpected death came, there was a fortification and a stability I would not have known otherwise.

I don't want to suggest though, that we should keep looking

back on past moments of spiritual victory. It's important for me to keep my relationship with God thoroughly fresh and up-to-date. I believe he has something new for me right now as I live expectantly. However, I am forced to look back so that I can clearly see the pathway perfectly laid out step by step to take me to the moment of crisis.

In taking the time to look back, I find a deep gratefulness in my heart once again for the unmatched love of God. His great, magnificent heart and his all-powerful help and healing are continuously available. His resources never run dry, there is always more and more and more.

For ten years I have enjoyed a revival of interest in reading books by authors who know Christ. Eugenia Price, Ruth Paxson, Watchman Nee, Stuart Briscoe, John Hunter, Ian Thomas, Paul Tournier, Lehman Strauss, Elisabeth Elliot are some of them. Roy Hession's little books have been especially valuable. The reading of all this good material was building my faith, enlarging my vision, filling me with God's great and immeasurable love. I was being prepared and I didn't know it.

During the summer of 1970, I read two books which were most unusual in a particular sense. I had no expectation of tragedy, yet I was motivated to read these books which would prove to be invaluable in the days so near. One was Paul Rees's *Triumphant in Trouble,* a study on suffering. The other was *Blessings out of Buffetings* by Alan Redpath. Can you explain why I would read those kinds of books? It had to be a God-arranged study to help ready me with strength and understanding for the time when they would be so necessary.

Bob and I have been blessed with many wonderful friends. We honestly do not understand what it means to be friendless.

Friends are not only a beautiful part of life and a precious gift from God, but I am convinced we need them constantly. The Greek philosopher Theophrastus said, "True friends visit us in prosperity only when invited, but in adversity they come without invitation." Our friends certainly proved their true friendship to us.

The one event we are most thankful for in God's program of development for testing is that he brought Diane home safely on Labor Day weekend. If the only word we had received after her letter of August telling us to "leave her alone" was the telegram revealing her death, how much more difficult it would have been to accept her death. God knew what was just ahead for all of us, and he graciously allowed us two wonderful months together. What more could we ask? There were the times we took walks together through the falling leaves. Diane had said, "This is the one time of year I miss in California, the fall. I am so glad to be home during this season." There was time to talk and talk. We had so much to share and so much to catch up on. What a warm and loving relationship it was. There were unexpected hugs and expressions of love. I can only say, "Thank you, God, for something beautiful."

During her two months at home, Diane made it a point to visit members of the family often, and she enjoyed Sand Point a few times. We have her singing voice on tape as well as her speaking voice. How we value this. I often visualize her as she was, healthy and lovely. We would catch glimpses of the glow and sparkle she had formerly lost coming back. And my heart says, "Thank you, dear God. It might have been so different. You knew what was ahead and brought her safely to us for a short while to enjoy." My heart grows even more grateful realizing she had exposed herself to extreme danger hitchhiking all the way from California. She traveled many miles on the back of a motorcycle with a stranger. The heels of her boots were burned to the sole from the exhaust system. She slept in her sleeping bag at night near the roadside and developed a cold and serious ear infection. Yet, through all these seeming dangers, she reached us safe and unharmed. God knew we needed this time together, for it would be our last. In our thinking, it was a miracle of God's love that she got safely home for those two beautiful months.

In looking back over the time preceding Diane's death, I can see a steady and continual work of God in her behalf as well as our behalf. He was preparing us all for November 17, 1970.

9.
Reflections

As I think of the steady and faithful help God has given us when we needed him the most, I wonder, "What do others do in their darkest hour when they don't have a personal relationship with God?" I have read of some who completely fall apart with emotional and mental breakdowns. Others grow bitter, hateful and rebellious. Still others launch revenge campaigns, and some have been known to actually grieve themselves to death. I have found that only God can sustain and hold together individual lives in such an hour.

I have read some outstanding testimonies of those who have suffered losses of loved ones—J. Hudson Taylor, Elisabeth Elliot, Catherine Marshall, Dale Evans Rogers. God helped each one in a completely individual way to meet every need. Some of these people had one tragic heartbreak piled right on top of another tragic heartbreak—and God always met the need!

Someone once suggested to me that Dale Evans Rogers was far more comforted and strengthened than I because of the many prayers for her. Since I was virtually unknown, few people by comparison were praying for me so I received less comfort. I didn't have to think about that too long at all. Dr. Cox has said many times that "there are no unimportant people with God." I realized that it is God who is the important one, not fame or popularity. It is God who does the dispensing of all the grace and strength we require in our times of crisis, no matter who the individuals are that need it. None of us are unimportant to him.

I admit to genuine suffering. The fact that I was a Christian did not lessen the pain. I could not gloss over the heartache in the guise of belonging to God, for this would have been entirely unrealistic. I couldn't smile and say, "Diane is in Heaven now and all her troubles are over, how I thank the Lord!" and then go about singing his praises. In fact, the "song of praise" eluded me for many days. Being overwhelmed with grief was my very human reaction—God understood it. The all-important factor was that I knew God was in it also—helping, caring, loving as it was needed; giving grace enough for each minute of the day. It truly worked out just that way, all I needed!

Life seemed impertinent at first. It stood right up and marched straight on leaving us behind. How could the world be so cold and unfeeling. I wanted to put reins on life and hold it back. I clutched at the past wanting to hold Diane near, but time wouldn't wait. The past kept getting farther and farther away. Then slowly, as emotions became more balanced again, I could see the wisdom of God. The painful event must recede and become more dim. Without that, healing could never take place. Our hearts were handed over to God and one of his wonder-ways is the using of time for our healing. Thank you, God.

I miss Diane still and no doubt I always shall. It is true I could not wish her back. She has experienced some wonderful months of untold bliss and I can be honest when I say I am glad for this. In the meantime, I have been experiencing tremendous and continuous healing. There is a deep sense (not possibly always evident) of joy and peace. With God's help I will live this day for him, and then the next day, until my last day. Then I'll begin a new life not only living *for* him but *with* him. And the healing will be complete.

I made an important discovery in those first days and nights following Diane's death. Upon retiring, and at other times as well, Satan managed to portray vividly and dramatically on the screen of my mind the entire appalling episode of Diane's murder. This could derange any normal mother. I deplored having this scene overdeveloped and amplified, then stretched across my mental vision. But there it was each time I closed my eyes. The facts were dreadful enough; these elaborations I didn't need.

I made a wonderful discovery, although it shouldn't have surprised me at all. God had been providing more than sufficient grace and strength for every situation, so why would I overlook the fact that he could help me here? With God's help I have found it is possible to deliberately pick up my thoughts and place them on him! It can be done. It takes discipline, yes, and constant repetition at first. I had to act on this many times in a single hour and for days! Gradually these attacks on my mind became fewer and fewer, and one day I suddenly became aware that they were haunting me no longer.

I do have an occasional flashback, but no real problem at all. Again, thank you, dear God.

For a number of years now, as I've mentioned, I have been absorbed with the idea of living *now* for God—this day, not tomorrow but now. Diane's death has added an urgency to the right-now living. After all, I have experienced deeply the truth that we do not know about our next hour. "For what is your life? It is even a vapor, that appeareth for a little time, and then vanisheth away" (James 4:14). At 9:15 P.M. as

Diane was seen near a lighted intersection in San Diego, she had no clue that within a half hour she would no longer be alive physically.

Most of us live as though we believe this life on earth will endure forever. But when someone close to us dies suddenly, especially someone as young as Diane, we realize that life is no idle gift. How important it is that we use life wisely and to full capacity. We may not have much of it left at all. Death is inevitable—there is no escaping it. We may like to bury our heads in the sand and simply not face death, but "it has been appointed unto man once to die." We don't know just when the sudden cutting off may be, but it will come.

I cannot expect our experience to have the same effect on everyone else. I have a strong desire, however (which I try to control), to get out the message, "Please be on the alert to the now of life. Do not wait to be all that you know you should be. Today is the day to live for Christ. Now is the time to help your neighbor, to love your sister, your brother, for tomorrow may be too late. Be grateful for each breath you breathe. Develop a thankful attitude. Be sensitive to the voice of the Holy Spirit within you as he guides through the temptations and conflicts, joys and ecstasies of today. Ask God to help you end your day a better person than you were at the beginning." Life is worth living in full, and right now!

At the time of Diane's death, Bob and I did much introspection and we made some promises to God and to each other. I believe Diane was taken for a purpose in God's great overall plan, and we were part of that plan. He wants to make use of our pain to bring forth something fresh, sweet and beautiful from our lives that was not there before: a clearer understanding of himself, a new love for him and for others, a desire to willingly give ourselves to him in every area. We want him to use our lives to glorify himself in his way and every day. This can only happen when we get ourselves out of the way and let God accomplish it.

As time marches on and the pain recedes, the tears aren't so frequent. As pleasant memories replace the tragic loss, there is a tendency to forget the commitments that were honestly made when our hearts were so tender and hurting. I don't believe in being unduly obsessed with death. However, I am certain that occasional reflecting on our crisis and reviewing our responses and promises is a good thing. Often as the difficulty becomes more dim, so do the commitments. This seems a dangerous thing to me, for God had trusted us with this heart anguish. What a trust! We dare not let him down. We must let him accomplish through us what he desires.

The Bible says, "These trials are only to test your faith, to see whether or not it is strong and pure. It is being tested as fire tests gold and purifies it—and your faith is far more precious to God than mere gold; so if your faith remains strong after being tried in the test tube of fiery trials, it will bring you much praise and glory and honor on the day of his return" (I Pet. 1:7, LB). I pray that my faith, after its testing, will bring praise and honor to my Lord.

"He that loveth his brother abideth in the light, and there is none occasion of stumbling in him."   1 John 2:10

10.
Burdens

I *have discovered that God has another way of using the* suffering and pain in my life. The Apostle Paul describes it this way:

> What a wonderful God we have—he is the Father of our Lord Jesus Christ, the source of every mercy, and the one who so wonderfully comforts and strengthens us in our hardships and trials. And why does he do this? So that when others are troubled, needing our sympathy and encouragement, we can pass on to them this same help and comfort God has given us. You can be sure the more we undergo sufferings for Christ, the more he will shower us with his comfort and encouragement. We are in deep trouble for bringing you God's comfort and salvation. But in our trouble God had comforted us—and this, too, to help you: to show you from our personal experience how God will tenderly comfort you when you undergo these same sufferings. He will give you strength to endure (2 Cor. 1:3–7, LB).

Paul's language stimulates me: "God wonderfully strengthens . . . he tenderly comforts . . . he showers us with encouragement."

For we have not an high priest which cannot be touched with
the feeling of our infirmities. . . . Let us therefore come boldly
unto the throne of grace, that we may obtain mercy, and find
grace to help in time of need (Heb. 4:15–16).

This, then, is one of God's great purposes. I do not understand another's crisis unless it has touched my life, or I have
gone through a similar experience. But having had the experience, it becomes my privilege and responsibility to share the
burdens of others. Because I have been there, I know and
understand what they are going through. I want to relate a
few instances of how God has been making it possible for some
of us to share together in this very special way.

Some time ago in the Detroit area, a beautiful seventeen-
year-old girl vanished. Three weeks later the girl's body was
uncovered in an area not too many miles away from her home.
She had been sexually attacked, brutally and unmercifully
killed. Bob and I watched the televised reports and read the
newspapers with sympathy and deep understanding. These be-
reaved parents also had an unwavering faith in God, and their
words and actions were a tremendous witness for Christ to the
entire area. How well Bob and I could relate to this. We could
see the courage, but we knew the anguish of their hearts.

I kept thinking of the parents and of their alone moments,
particularly after the first bewildering days of bereavement
were past. I knew so well what they were experiencing. Though
they were strangers to us, I sat down one day and wrote them
a letter expressing our understanding and love. I shared what
had happened in our lives, how God had given the needed
grace and strength, and assured them of our constant prayer
for God's gracious touch of healing on their broken hearts.

The mother called one day soon after she had received the
letter. She told me of the tremendous amount of mail they
had received and of the responses from hundreds of people
whose hearts had been deeply touched by the tragedy. We were
the only ones, however, who had gone through a similar loss.

They knew that we, of all people, truly understood their grief.

A lovely friendship has developed between us. We needed each other. In our mutual pain we have been a strength to each other, and now, each in turn, to others. Their mail and phone constantly bring pleas for help from acutely grief-stricken people, and now they too minister in this new way. It is one of God's gracious ways of supplying what we need in such an hour.

I met another lady in a church parking lot one day. I had been told that only three months previously she and her husband had lost their only daughter, aged nineteen. Yet there she stood looking radiant and praising the Lord. Although we didn't talk about it then, I felt sure that behind the smile there was a broken heart. I also was confident there were difficult alone days, since their daughter had been gone only three short months. I spent time praying for my new friend, and one day God gave me the courage to call her on the phone. I shared our experience with her. She, in turn, bared her heart regarding their loss.

"We didn't feel we should sadden others by our grief," my friend said, "as we were now experiencing God's all-sufficient grace and strength. This was made possible only through the Holy Spirit and the prayers of God's people. We wanted our lives to show forth his praises so others could see that God was real and the power was not of ourselves."

Oh, surely, they experienced pain of the deepest sort, a hurt that only God himself thoroughly understands. And, to be completely honest, a kind of wound that never entirely disappears. In the process of ongoing time there is positive healing, true. Life would be extremely crippled and far from normal if the mending sutures could never be removed from our hearts by our great Physician. They can be and are. Yet the scars remain, and when surface matters are pushed aside a bit upon a moment of reflection, the sting is there—a sensitiveness that is unmistakable! However, our supreme Heart Specialist fills our minds and lives with much which has significance along with more knowledge of himself and the "moments of reflection" become fewer. In exchange for this "sensitiveness," his peace is a balm for our refreshing and assuaging.

My friend, in her quiet, behind-the-scenes way, is constantly reaching out in compassion and help to others who need God's encouragement, praying for them, writing letters and appropriate cards along with Scriptures, poems and gospel tracts.

God knew my friend and I needed each other and arranged the whole meeting, I am convinced. We enjoy being together, and because we have a mutual understanding deep in our hearts, it has been easy to share some of the great and wonderful things God is constantly teaching us. I count her a valuable person in my life, and it is because God knew our need for each other!

Some time ago an acquaintance came to me for help and spiritual guidance. During our conversations I related some of the incidents and insights surrounding Diane's death and shared our experience of God's grace and help at that time. This friend was a fairly new Christian, and God had been opening her eyes to many valuable biblical truths she had not understood before. She was growing tremendously.

Then one morning she awakened to find her twenty-one-year-old son dead—of carbon monoxide poisoning! I knew her world went crumbling in an instant. A few days after the funeral, my friend put her arm around me and said, "I knew you understood completely. I never would have made it if God had not taught me through you. What you shared with me during our conversations is what helped me so much during these especially difficult days. I could look at you and remember what God had done for your family, and it gave me confidence that the same God would do this for me and my family, and he has."

All of these instances have enriched my life. They have

given me larger vision and clearer insights as to how God works. He knows what he is doing. We really do help one another because of our shared suffering, and we become richer for helping. God has planned it all, and in love.

Only recently three separate requests came our way that we try to help and encourage three couples who had lost daughters in similar circumstances. Some have not responded, but perhaps they have to God, and that is what matters. Besides, one person can't be stretched all across the nation to give assistance and help. God has his people placed strategically. Therefore when some special person needs understanding and caring during a crisis time, the right people are in the right places for God's using in this way. I am learning how to release these burdens, knowing that God has other persons closer at hand geographically, who can be of much greater help in a consistent way than I could ever be.

To help others cope with tragedy and grief is a ministry I feel God is opening and leading us into, one we could never have understood a few years ago. I pray for a continued warmth, sensitiveness and responsiveness to these acute emotional needs. I want to be always ready to dispense the compassion and love of our great and wonderful God.

> *"To open their eyes and to turn them from darkness to light, and from the power of Satan unto God, that they may receive forgiveness of sins."* Acts 26:18

11.
Forgive the Murderer?

*D*ispensing *the love of God to people who have gone* through tragedy similar to ours is one thing. But what about the murderer of our daughter? Could we show him love?

After the San Diego county coroner had given my husband all the nightmarish details of Diane's death, we soon learned a little of how the world reacted to such a crime. We already knew in a way, but now we were dealing with it firsthand.

The news of murder spreads like wildfire. Overnight it seemed as though everyone knew. Our neighbors and friends were shocked, up in arms and angered, though they were compassionate and heartbroken for us. We were told in no uncertain terms that we should be on our way to California to "track down that rapist-murderer maniac and tear him limb from limb."

At the time, understandably, we scarcely heard what people were saying. Later, as the numbing effects were disappearing and we began mentally functioning again, we were appalled at the ruthless and heartless response demanded of us. And yet, hadn't our daughter been ruthlessly and heartlessly murdered?

Yes, she had. We hated the murder intensely. It was a hor-

rible act of injustice done to our daughter, a violent and blame-
worthy crime. It was ugly, heinous, unfair, and it tore us apart.
We despised the way in which Diane had been brutally handled
and strangled. The marks on her body showed that she fought,
and fought hard—thus her death, perhaps? But though we
thoroughly and completely despised the manner in which she
died, we found that we did not despise the one who did it. We
desperately hated the killing, but we did not and do not hate
the killer. We did want to see him apprehended, but only because we did not care to have any murderer free to harm in-
nocent persons.

We have suffered tremendous physical and emotional loss,
but God has allowed us to keep in focus the preciousness and
importance of the killer's eternal soul, knowing that God loves
and sacrificed himself for him. We began almost immediately
to pray for him daily. If God could use the very crime he committed to be the means of drawing him to salvation from his
sin, what greater miracle could we ever expect to hope for?

None of this seemed to make a whole lot of sense to many
people. Frankly, we didn't understand it too well ourselves.
We just knew that this is very honestly how it was. But to our
further amazement, we began to realize that some of our
Christian friends, who shared the same faith in God that we
had, were having very real difficulties with their attitudes toward Diane's killer. I began to do some more sorting of my
own thoughts. It looked as though God had performed a
miracle in our hearts. Rather than being filled with malice and
venom, we were filled with great concern and caring about
what happened to this man, whoever and wherever he was.

Approximately two and a half years after Diane's death, we
received a phone call from the San Diego district attorney.
Diane's killer had been apprehended, brought to trial and con-
victed for first-degree murder. He was sentenced to double life
imprisonment—one sentence for murder and one for rape.
Suddenly he became a known rather than an unknown figure
—a real person not an abstract form. Now we could pray for

him by name. Our desire that God would reach him increased.

In the latter part of the summer of 1975, Bob and I made a trip West. Prison Missions Association, Inc., of Riverside, California, was on our agenda, because we wanted to get them in touch with Diane's murderer. The people at Prison Missions were wonderful to us, and we were deeply impressed with their Christ-centered outreach to prison inmates all across the United States and in other parts of the world. When we told them that we wanted this prisoner to know of our love and concern and of God's great plan for his life through Jesus Christ, even they thought our request was a rare one. But they started immediately on the proper procedures to make the contact.

The director of Prison Missions made the contact himself. Knowing that the gospel had been shared with the killer was indeed the pinnacle of our entire trip. We had seen many spectacular views—the grandeur of the mountains, clear sparkling streams gushing through crevices and dropping noisily over precipices to the bottom of canyons—all truly breathtaking and awe-inspiring. But none could top knowing that the first step had been taken in sharing God's love with a special person.

We quickly wrote a few notes to special friends, sharing this wonderful thing God was allowing us to be involved in and asking them to help us pray for this one so special to God who so desperately needs Christ in his heart and life. We were a bit disillusioned at first to discover that some of our friends found they could not help us in this way. They had tried, but said it was almost impossible to pray for him. One person said, "I'm sorry, I just can't feel the way you do. I hope he gets all he's got coming to him and then some." I was quick to state that certainly the murderer has a great debt to pay. We were praying, though, for his release from sin through the redemptive work of Christ who has already so graciously paid the great debt. Only then will he be a free person!

As I thought on the difficulties our friends were having, I began to understand something much more clearly. God had preconditioned our hearts for a man whom he knew would be thrust into our lives, thrown right across our path in the midst of unusual circumstances. We believed he should not be ignored. The hearts of our friends did not need this kind of conditioning. This man would not become their responsibility. It made it easier for me to understand and accept their problem. It was all right that they could not help us pray—I could see it now. But this young man has become our responsibility, so we continue to pray for him. We can see no other purpose for his coming into our lives if there is no possibility that he will be saved. God has special plans for his life, I know, and to be allowed to stand on the sidelines and observe God's transforming power at work is a privilege. The experience has had a subduing and quieting effect on us, almost as though we were walking on holy ground, somewhat fearful to make a move lest God's plan be thwarted.

When our friend said, "I hope he gets all that is coming to him," I thought that in one sense this prisoner is already on death row. The Bible tells us that "it is appointed unto men once to die, but after this the judgment" (Heb. 9:27), and that "at the name of Jesus every knee should bow . . . and that every tongue should confess that Jesus Christ is Lord, to the glory of God the Father" (Phil. 2:10, 11). None of us will escape this appointment with death when we meet our Maker face to face. Our desire is that this young man may not experience eternal death, but rather, eternal life through Jesus Christ our Lord (Rom. 6:23).

By the time we arrived home from vacation, there was already a letter here waiting from Prison Missions. They had received a quick response to their letter and had sent us a copy. The prisoner was deeply touched with the message conveyed to him and wanted to know if he could write to us directly via the Mission. The director suggested that we correspond in this way if we felt we wanted to.

One of the most joyful and yet difficult compositions I have ever put together was that first letter. It had to be worded carefully and filled with love and understanding as much as possible. We did not, in any way, want him to believe we condoned the crime committed against our daughter, against us, and against God. We did, in every way, want him to believe that we were concerned for him and cared very much about what happened to him. And above all else, that God was concerned and cared and was anxiously waiting to save him from his sin through the death of his Son, Jesus Christ. God has endowed each person with a will to choose for himself whether he will receive or reject the Son of God. So as best I knew how, with the Holy Spirit's help, I wrote the letter, sealed it and dropped it into the mail, knowing that it went wrapped securely in God's love and our prayers—and a little bit of fear and trembling.

After a few weeks, we began hoping for a response. None came. Several more weeks slipped by, and then I began to think how I might react if I were in his shoes. The results were revealing. I could envision the emotional shock involved in receiving a letter from the parents of the girl he had killed, especially when it was in no way filled with bitterness or anger—which he might have expected. "How do I react? How on the level are these people? What motivates them? Is it for my good or bad? Am I sticking my neck out in becoming involved? They have made a sudden invasion into my life. How do I handle it? How can I, the murderer, write to the parents of the one I killed? Can I trust them?" I began to see how difficult, if not impossible, it might be for him to respond at all.

I prepared a second letter explaining that we could understand his hesitancy in writing and his possible feeling of uneasiness in trusting us. "It is all right" I said, "if you feel you cannot write to us, but we are interested in keeping in touch with you."

About the middle of January we received his first direct communication. I sat weeping. Not because he had eagerly opened his heart to receive Christ. He hadn't, not yet anyway.

Only God knows when this special person will do that. But, just the fact he had responded at all seemed like a miracle. There was evidence that his heart had been deeply touched. He was beginning to do some serious thinking about God, and was seeing that just possibly Christianity does work after all, even though he had not been much of a believer in God. He expressed gratitude for having met us through our letters; our kindnesses to him had hurt, yet were comforting. He hadn't realized there were people in the world anywhere who would place their concern for him above their own deep hurt. He could scarcely take it in and had been sharing it with his fellow associates.

All the incidents of the past few years, he said, including losing his young wife and child through divorce, had brought him to an all-time low. As he reviewed his life he didn't like what he saw and realized that it called for change. "To be truthful, I find it extremely difficult to communicate my good feelings for you. You have set a wonderful example, one that has greatly inspired me. It is beautiful and effective. I take great pleasure in telling my friends of the truly sincere people that I have met. . . ."

Since his first letter, some of the Prison Missions personnel have been to his prison to minister. When he learned of their coming, he made a special request that the chaplain allow him to visit personally with the director of the Mission who has been in touch with him by letter, tapes and literature. His request was granted. This is encouraging to us, for we know that his interest in knowing about God and his plan to save is becoming greater.

We view this young man as a person of value and importance to God. After all he was made in the image of God. According to Genesis 9:6 this is what places value on human life as far as God is concerned, and he desires our fellowship. One wonderful day this valuable person will place his faith in God and in his Son. I'm hoping it will be soon.

To realize that God is using a tragic experience several years ago that affected us deeply, so that he can perform something very beautiful in the life of a special person today is viewing real live drama in motion by God, right before our eyes. We can hardly take this in. It has moved our family deeply. It has given us an increasing understanding of and respect for the methods and the time span involved in the working out of God's plan in our lives. I am constantly amazed by the varied and completely unexpected ways in which God accomplishes his fantastic work. He is never overstrained, rushing to meet deadlines, punching a time clock, nor are his energies overtaxed. I have had my pet theories and I have often been guilty of telling God how to do things, and the precise way he should answer my prayers. Or sometimes I have simply assumed he will act thus and so! Then right out of the blue, he begins to unfold his plan—entirely diametric to mine—and his way always proves to be best. Why would I ever assume the responsibility of telling God what to do and how? I learn so slowly. However, to be privileged to watch him move and work gives my faith a tremendous boost. It also gives me a fresh awareness of his sovereignty and grace. He will step right over my well-thought-out (yet foolish) plans and perform his miracles of love and at the right time, in spite of me. What a God!

We have never really questioned God for having taken Diane home so early in her life. We have felt we have not needed answers or reasons. We have, by God's grace, been able to trust him, that he makes no mistakes. Still, in his love and caring about how we feel, he is lifting the curtain just a wee bit to show us at least one of his special reasons, and this gives us just a little more understanding of Diane's death. We do not need to understand, but he is showing us anyway.

I mentioned earlier that we didn't hate or despise Diane's killer. The temptation to hate is always there. But just suppose that I did have deep resentments and hatred for the one who killed Diane. From some points of view I would have every right to hold such attitudes. It would be normal. To what lengths could my bitterness take me? I could strike back, write threatening letters filled with deadly poison, make all kinds of vindictive statements and truly be "out to get him" one evil way or another. "I'll pay him back! I'll get even with him if it is the last thing I do."

None of this could touch the young man in prison other than to make him still more bitter toward life, and people, and God. It would most certainly not bring our precious daughter back, and it would have an inner destroying effect on my own life. I would be doing harm only to myself. One writer states that malice not only spreads but also destroys all that is noble in a person's life. It is blind and knows nothing but to disparage good qualities. The dictionary associates malice with malignancy—it eats and consumes and finally destroys. If I allow it to take hold in my life, I am anything but a free person. The very tool I would use to get even is the one that would chain me. Only God is able to handle this kind of treachery in our lives and release us from the entrapment.

Personal revenge is forbidden in the Scriptures. "Dearly beloved, avenge not yourselves, but rather give place unto wrath: for it is written, Vengeance is mine; I will repay, saith the Lord" (Rom. 12:19). Then again: "Finally, be ye all of one mind, having compassion one of another; love as brethren, be pitiful, be courteous: Not rendering evil for evil, or railing for railing. . . . For the face of the Lord is against them that do evil" (1 Pet. 3:8–9, 12). In other words, if I insist on revenge, I will be allowed to mess things up, make a bad matter worse and be a completely miserable person while doing it. Or I can turn the whole affair over to God and be freed of its burden and the weight that is killing me. I can let God handle it, justly and fairly. He knows the intentions of a man's heart. He understands all the circumstances better than I ever could. He will do right; I don't have to bother with it. What a relief!

So the decision is mine. I either carry anger, unforgiveness, resentment around with me, and break under the load, or, hand it over to my Heavenly Father who can bear the weight so easily. His promises are true, he will repay, I don't have to do it. I can let go, begin to breathe again, and live and grow.

However, God in his love and mercy has provided for every person a way out of sin's condemnation. "For God so loved the world, that he gave his only begotten Son, that whosoever believeth in him should not perish, but have everlasting life" (John 3:16).

I'm not, however, claiming now to be the epitome of forgiveness. Neither do I pretend to be the authority regarding it. In these unusual circumstances it seems that God has given me a forgiving spirit, and I can't tell you how glad I am. But how do I know for sure about the future? I am human and subject to any and all temptation, just like anyone else. Some incident of much less consequence could develop and a spirit of unforgiveness rear its ugly head. It could be out there somewhere ahead of me, to battle against and to deal with, I don't know. But I do know that it is possible to be able to freely forgive. If it is happening here, then I can certainly trust God for this kind of spirit in most any and every kind of circumstance.

God himself has set an effective example. "As far as the east is from the west, so far hath he removed our transgressions from us" (Ps. 103:12). "I have blotted out, as a thick cloud, thy transgressions, and, as a cloud, thy sins" (Isa. 44:22). He forgets them too (Isa. 43:25). Demonstrating the heart of his Father, on the cross, in the midst of the most brutal physical punishment and torment, Jesus Christ was enabled to say, "Father, forgive them, for they know not what they do." And so forgiveness is required of us: "Let all bitterness, and wrath, and anger, and clamor, and evil speaking, be put away from you, with all malice: And be ye kind one to another, tenderhearted, forgiving one another, even as God, for Christ's sake, hath forgiven you" (Eph. 4:31, 32).

Though we fail so miserably, along with Christ's admonitions come his enablings, and it is possible to forgive. I am grateful that is so.

"The god of this world hath blinded the
minds of them which believe not, lest the
light of the glorious gospel of Christ, who
is the image of God, should shine unto
them."   2 Corinthians 4:4

12.
Observations

As I mentioned in chapter 2, during her last year of high
school, Diane began having doubts about herself and her faith.
She believed she must search for truth and find answers independently. Were her beliefs a result of her own thinking or
had they been forced on her? What was life all about for her,
and what was its purpose, if any?

Diane asked me once, "Mom, didn't you ever question? Did
you always simply believe everything your Mom and Dad believed without wanting to take it apart and examine it to see if
if was for real?" I thought about that for a few minutes, and
then answered with what I honestly thought was the truth:
"Yes, I guess I did believe. It made the right kind of sense for
me and was the answer to my particular needs. Oh, my thinking
has changed down through the years regarding the right and
wrong of incidental things, but the basics, the fundamental
teaching of Scripture, I readily believed." Diane pensively
shook her head as if it was almost too much to believe.

Later, after Diane's death, I was looking over some old papers
I had saved, including some of my teen thoughts, and I was

caught short! "I am passing through a terrible period spiritually," I had written when I was about nineteen.

I am afraid to talk it over with my parents. I am becoming
frightened of night beauty—like a full moon. It is like God's
searchlight shining deeply into my very soul. Northern lights,
with their mystical and varicolored light rays constantly inter-
twining. They are awesome and appear to be a tower to Heaven,
a cathedral in the skies, and I am scared to death! These things
bring vividly to mind the return of Christ for some reason, and
this alarms me a whole lot. Why? Aren't I ready to meet him
when he comes? I know I have received Christ into my heart. I
can't even pray—God is so far away. When I go to church I
feel like a big hypocrite, just going through the motions of being a happy Christian, and I have a strong dislike for hypocrisy.

It was all the devil's lie—he was placing doubts and fears
into my mind. But through struggling along that particular
summer, and being reinforced by the promises in God's Word,
these hang-ups were finally overcome. I have often thought
Diane would have liked knowing about that struggle. It would
have seemed more realistic to her than simply blandly acqui-
escing without question.

Diane's search for something to fill the God-shaped need in
her continued for several years. Evidence for this came to us
when her personal belongings reached home after her death.
Among her possessions were many books on the different cults
and religions of our day. These spoke volumes to me of just
how intense her search was. As I looked over those books, there
was a genuine ache in my heart.

One book explained religious meditation and its varied
methods and values. Another dealt with mysticism, extrasensory
perception, and how to become "spirit-sphere attuned." I found
a set of rites and rituals and exercises to make one spiritual and
to cleanse one's life. I read of transcendentalism—going beyond
anything realizable in human experience.

All the cults and religions set forth in Diane's books could
never fill the emptiness within her heart. As I read, I longed

to put my arms around her—to remind her of God's great love and his truth.

Dr. Cox has said, "Our baffling questions and searchings for truth are indeed tragic. The total answer is realistically before us, and we do not have the eyes to see that it is Jesus Christ himself." Diane had apparently forgotten that Christ was with her constantly, always ready to clear her confused thinking, free her of hang-ups and help her make sense out of life. He would never force his way into her life, but he was—and is—available.

Jesus said about himself, "I am the way, the truth and the life; no man cometh unto the Father [God] but by me" (John 14:6). If Diane had kept her belief and trust centered in him, he could have filled the void and supplied the needs of her searching heart. The Bible talks about a "way that seemeth right unto a man, but the end thereof are the ways of death" (Prov. 16:25). Many ways that seem right were described in Diane's books, but they didn't recognize the truth of God. Jesus himself said that anyone who didn't enter by the door (himself) into the sheepfold is a thief and a robber.

The great thief and robber is Satan, and he tries to persuade us to bypass Jesus Christ. He is our greatest enemy, and it is dangerous to underestimate his power. The Bible calls him the god of this age, the prince of the power of the air, an angel of light deceiving many. He wants to baffle, confuse and mislead us regarding true values in life, and to distort our thinking regarding Jesus Christ.

It is difficult to understand, though, how we can be blinded again once our eyes have been opened to our need for Christ and we have received him into our life. Yet we know that Satan is the father of lies. He tested Jesus who was perfect, so how can we expect to escape? He is capable of perverting Scripture (Matt. 4:6), so why would he not try to distort our minds? He attacked Job severely, and Job was an upright man who reverenced God. He enticed David to disobey God (1 Chron. 21:1). Peter tell us to "be sober, be vigilant; because

your adversary the devil, as a roaring lion, walketh about,
seeking whom he may devour." The devil is skilled in deluding
our thinking and causing us to question the validity of our
faith. He succeeded with Diane. Only God the Holy Spirit
could reawaken her understanding and make her sensitive to
the fact that Jesus Christ could be more than she could ever
need.

I am aware of Satan's terrifying sway and his all-encircling
scope and sweep. He has many devices, philosophies, religions
and mind-manipulating schemes to attract attention, and he
succeeds. There is a disturbing increase in demon worship, an
almost unbelievable growth in the "Synagogue of Satan" (Rev.
2:9, 3:9), and an intense revival of the occult. Today's youth
culture is deep into free sex. These facts are not new but are
now completely open and accepted as a normal way of life.
There are some existing situations far worse than death. Diane
could have possibly become ensnared in something completely
devastating! She is now safe from all of it!

One of Diane's former friends, Jill, recently told us of a
young man who had just taken his life. He had been practicing astroprojection and was living above this material world
in the spirit-sphere. He had been spending so much of his time
in this escapism that "he didn't have time to take proper care
of his physical body or the needs of his family," she said. So
he made the decision to end his life on earth. His own thing
had gripped him in such a way that he could not cope with
life here in time as we know it.

In Ephesians 6:11–12, Paul writes this warning: "Put on
all of God's armor so that you will be able to stand safe against
all strategies and tricks of Satan. For we are not fighting against
people made of flesh and blood, but against persons without
bodies—the evil rulers of the unseen world, those mighty
satanic beings and great evil princes of darkness who rule this
world; and against huge numbers of wicked spirits in the spirit
world" (LB).

Many routes have been taken in the search for freedom and

truth. It finally became logical to Diane to accept the simple truth of God as he has set it forth in Jesus Christ and she came back to this, thank God. Diane found the freedom she had been searching for, and a release from the guilt which had plagued her. She was only beginning to discover boundless freedom in the grace of God and to open the door to a whole new and exciting dimension of abundant life in Christ. Although her physical life came to an abrupt end so soon after she was being liberated, the glories and freedom of eternity are hers forever. She has found, I know, that Jesus Christ is the answer to her questions.

"This then is the message which we have heard of him and declare unto you, that God is light and in him is no darkness at all."

1 John 1:5

13.
Questions

Some of Diane's friends have had very real and honest questions since her death. They have been dubious and skeptical of the goodness of God. This is understandable. I see the big question mark myself occasionally. Let me share my thinking regarding some of their questions.

One friend has doubtingly asked, "Can anyone ever really understand what God is all about? Some things he supposedly permits seem completely unfair to me. I find it extremely difficult to accept what he has let happen."

I, personally, do not believe that God and the man responsible for Diane's death were in collaboration. I am certain God could have diverted the treacherous act, and he chose not to. He is not liable, however, for the evil way she died. This is what seems difficult for some to accept; yet evil is totally against God's nature. James 1:13–15 records that "when someone wants to do wrong it is never God who is tempting him, for God never wants to do wrong and never tempts anyone else to do it. Temptation is the pull of man's own evil thoughts and wishes. These evil thoughts lead to evil actions and afterwards to the death penalty from God" (LB). From

God's viewpoint, he is working out a general overall plan and purpose for each individual life, from before the foundation of the world (Eph. 1:4, 11; Rom. 8:28). I have accepted this as a small part of his great eternal purpose. Diane had completed his plan for her life here on earth, even though it is difficult to understand from the human viewpoint.

I am sure we can never understand God in his entirety. He is infinite and we are not. But I believe we can learn to know him more and more as we read of him in the Bible. The Bible shows us clearly that God is knowable. The picture becomes clearer as we look at him through his only Son who came to earth for the express purpose of putting God into understandable form. Christ became human, God in the flesh, and in doing this was able to display the tremendous love and grace of God. We could not have comprehended any of it if Christ had not been "made flesh and dwelt among us" (John 1:14). Jesus came so we may know God personally.

When I say that we can know God, I mean that we can explore some small areas of his love and grace—which are limitless and exhaustless. It is important to grasp such a profile of God. This comprehension can be gained only by reading and studying the Word of God. God's grace is unmeasurable (see Eph. 1:7). His blessings are countless. We are so important and valuable to him that he knows the exact number of hairs on our head (Luke 12:7). His love is so deep that he sacrificed the most beloved he had, his only Son, so that we might have an intimate relationship with him. His grace is so wide that no matter what we have done or thought, or where we may have gone, how far up or how far down, he loves us still.

He loved us enough to do something about the sin that separates us from him and keeps us from his holy and perfect presence. He became a human being. In Jesus Christ he became one of us—a flesh-and-blood man. Though he was sinless, he gave his life as a sacrifice for our sins, the sins of the whole world. He came to die in our place—to be our substitute. He was the only one in the universe who had the capacity to "bear our sins in his own body on the tree, that we, being dead to sins, should live unto righteousness, by whose stripes we were healed" (1 Pet. 2:24).

We'll never be able to comprehend the cost of Calvary to God, but we can begin to appreciate the depths of his love. I never look at the cross without seeing his overwhelming love for me. I can grasp a little of how compassionate his thoughts are toward me, and how great is the number of them. If I tried to count them, they would outnumber the sand (see Ps. 139:17–18). He loves me with an everlasting love; in loving kindness he has drawn me to himself (Jer. 31:3). We are of considerable importance, for God paid dearly to redeem us, "not with corruptible things as silver and gold, but with the precious blood of Christ, as of a lamb without blemish and without spot" (1 Pet. 1:18–19). This kind of God I want to really know!

If we understood everything about God, we would be bringing him down to our level and this would be sad. I am glad we cannot do it. I want the God in whom I place my trust and confidence to have "ways that are not my ways and thoughts that are past finding out"—"secrets that belong only to him" (Isa. 55:8–9; Deut. 29:29). But because I can comprehend a little of his heart of love for me, it becomes increasingly easy to let go of doubts and questions that plague, and simply trust him with all things.

A young person closely associated with Diane once said, "Placing our lives into the will and plan of God is defeatism. If we are nothing and there is no good in us, and our own righteousness is as filthy rags in God's sight, and if there is none righteous, no not one, then why bother at all? It is negativism. And, even if there might be some good in us, we have to surrender it all to God. We have lost before we have begun—it seems like defeatism to me." What an interesting thought process!

The concept here of what it means to be a Christian is not clearly understood, I would say. It is true, we can add nothing to the loving work of Calvary. In this area we are no good. We *have* all sinned and come short of the glory of God, and only God can remedy the situation. We can add nothing. But this does not, by any means, conclude that we are worthless.

It is psychologically true that we cannot be defeated and happy. Therefore, we will not readily subject ourselves to defeat. The Bible tells us that a person "should not think of himself more highly than he ought to think" (Rom. 12:3), but this does not mean that we shouldn't think well of ourselves —just "not more highly than we ought." God would never have paid the price he did if we were of no value to him. He made us in his own image—that speaks loudly to me that he made us worthwhile beings. He expects us to have respect for ourselves as persons—our integrity, capabilities and talents.

Jesus told us to love God with all our heart and soul, and strength and mind," and to love our neighbor as ourself (Luke 10:27). We can't love the people next door very much if we don't care about ourselves a little. Paul wrote, "For no man yet hated his own flesh; but nourisheth and cherisheth it" (Eph. 5:29). So God does expect us to experience some self-love. In fact, it is something we are born with—it is God-given.

Dare we think for a minute that God would have put himself and his Son through the tortures of the cross if he had not and does not see worth in us? He knows we have energies, talents and abilities. We are valuable to him. The fact is that when God's life invades our being through the Holy Spirit, a tremendously new and exciting dimension is added. Our capabilities, talents and energies become increasingly effective. We make a far greater contribution to society when God becomes our motivation. He steadfastly helps in the discipline of our will and mind, and we are determined to do what must be done. These qualities of discipline down deep within our lives do not lead to defeatism, but rather the making of strong, tall persons who become invaluable to God and man. The Christian life is not one of defeat. It is, in fact, the only life that wins!

Another of Diane's friends asks, "God would never ask us to deny ourselves, take up our cross and follow him, would he? This would destroy our identity and, since he gave it to us in the first place, it doesn't make sense that he would ask us to give it up."

In Matthew 16:24 Christ was talking with his disciples regarding his forthcoming death, trying to make them understand. It was more than they could comprehend and he knew it. The truth presented here in relating to identity is the identifying of ourselves with Christ in his death. This is exactly what takes place when we receive Christ as our Savior from sin. God the Holy Spirit baptizes us into Jesus Christ and we do become one in Christ. This does not destroy our individuality in any way.

God made each of us separate and distinct, to think and act independently. No two persons are alike, and this is as God meant it. Paul certainly did not lose his identity when he became a Christian. He was very much his own person, turning the world upside down. However, with all of his individualism he wrote:

> But all these things that I once thought very worthwhile—now I've thrown them all away so that I can put my trust and hope in Christ alone. Yes, everything else is worthless when compared with the priceless gain of knowing Christ Jesus my Lord. I have put aside all else, counting it worth less than nothing, in order that I can have Christ (Phil. 3:7–8, LB).

He wasn't thinking of it as denial in any way.

Peter was an impetuous, and often thoughtless individual. But he was completely willing to be an involved person, and was a powerful proponent of the gospel of Jesus Christ. He spoke up to the religious authorities, even after he had been thrown into prison, and said, "We ought to obey God rather than men" (Acts 5:29). In his first letter, we find him actually rejoicing and glorying in suffering for Christ (1 Peter 1:6–8). He had the positive aspect of denying himself in view. In fact, he did not look upon it as a denial of himself whatsoever. He still maintained his individualism, although he identified himself with Christ, as though they were one. This isn't difficult to understand, for we see the same principle in marriage. Two people are united and become one flesh, yet they remain two individual people.

John the Baptist never lost his unique identity. In his love and devotion to Jesus Christ, however, he said that Jesus "must become greater and greater, and I must become less and less" (John 3:30, LB). These men realized that in losing their lives for Christ, they would find them again in fuller and richer abundance. It truly happened just that way. Their lives overflowed with love and concern for mankind. They gave their lives in trying to show people the importance of identifying with Christ Jesus—nothing lost—all gain!

The men who wrote our Bible were distinct individuals. Some were educated and others not, yet God used them. They had different abilities and handicaps; God had not poured them into the same mold. From their varied walks and stations in life he worked through them and brought forth his Holy Word, the sacred Scriptures!

He will do this for every individual life that has been identified with him in his death and resurrection. He'll take each unique personality guided by his Spirit, not to make it like someone else, but to make it genuinely free. Our distinct and individual lives will touch other lives with God's love in a way that could not have been possible if we were like somebody else.

The phone rang one evening and another of Diane's friends confided, "I honestly dislike the now way of life with its looseness and so called freedom," he said. "In the working world, however, I am constantly confronted with it, and my values become shaky. I ask God to stabilize my faith and to give me courage to face the day in his strength. Yet, when I step into that world each morning, I find my courage falls away. I float through another day taking no stand at all for the things I believe in. How can I handle this problem?"

Dr. Cox says, "Drifting is the easiest, most delightful and effortless way of dying." We are living in a day of drifters— we float along with the tide because it's easier that way. This kind of thinking coming from today's down-to-earth and nonconforming young people seems unbelievable. They do not believe in what they are doing but are doing it anyway. Still, I do know that the outside pressures are strong.

As I mentioned in chapter 9, I am learning that it is possible to mentally decide to pick up one's thoughts and place them elsewhere deliberately. It takes a whole lot of practice. It may be necessary countless times in a day at first, but it can be done.

When our thoughts are drifting or being controlled by someone or something else, we can deliberately pick them up, to place them on our books, our jobs, our human relationships, our spiritual relationships. We can plan a course of action, and with the help of God, discipline our minds and make them obey as many times a day as is necessary, and ultimately we will be the winners. God will help us to finally be free persons, not drifters—free to stand for the God we believe in and for the kind of life God believes in. It is well worth the effort.

"And the peace of God which passeth all understanding will keep your hearts and minds through Christ Jesus our Lord" (Phil. 4:7).

"For ye were sometimes darkness, but now are ye light in the Lord: walk as children of light." Ephesians 5:8

14.
Sentimental Journey

*W*e had just observed Mother's Day and there were a few days before Diane's birthday. These special mother and daughter days, though not related, had revived cherished memories, and I was filled with a yearning to visit Diane's grave. I was hoping that on the windows of my mind there might be some reflections of beautiful past moments. I do not make this journey often.

It was a brilliant spring day. The recent rains had washed the earth clean, rinsing away the muck and grime of winter. The trees and bushes were bursting forth with life, with fragrance, with greenery. Even the cemetery, believe it or not, seemed alive. The caretakers had been cleaning away winter debris and mowing the grass in readiness for the forthcoming Memorial Day celebration. Fresh flowers had been planted on some of the graves, giving evidence of caring hearts.

I parked the car and began strolling about the grounds. I noticed from various grave markers that some had lived a fairly lengthy life span according to man's timetable. Others were very young when death claimed them from this life. Soberly I observed a freshly dug grave with a canopy protecting it. For one short moment I experienced acute anguish knowing someone, that very day, would be laying a loved one to rest.

Diane's gravestone reads very simply:

DIANE RUTH BRISTOL

Born May 22, 1949—Died November 17, 1970

Even now I can scarcely look at that cold marble slab, seeing her name inscribed there, and hold the tears back. It still seems unreal and impossible at times. True, the wounds have healed. I do not suffer nearly so much. But the scars remain sensitive, and there are moments of hurting which God understands.

I remembered one letter we had received at the time of Diane's death. "When we parents choose to have a family, it is one of the risks we all take, that of losing a precious child in death, and prematurely," my friend wrote. "Only think about the twenty-one years of enjoyment you would have been denied had Diane not been born." I gave God thanks right then and there for having given us the privilege of enjoying her for twenty-one years. I thanked him, too, for the promise of enjoying her again with him in eternity. What a precious and comforting hope!

As I stooped to pull some of the longer grass away from the marker, I reflected on the graciousness of my Heavenly Father and his unpredictable provisions always at the right moment to meet our prevailing need. Diane's body had been placed in the grave, right here before me a few years ago, on Monday, November 23rd, and Thanksgiving Day was just ahead. As a family, we were submerged in pain and agony and could not see then the future compensations God was shaping for us. He never leaves us unattended or unaided. We didn't have to fend for ourselves. He knew of our bereft state and had taken all kinds of preparatory measures, one upon another, to fill the frightening hollow space within. From the very beginning he became my personal *Hiding Place.* I wanted to shrink from everyone and everything else. It seemed I was only safe with him, and we were in constant touch. I didn't pray audibly. I was unable, really, to form words even in my spirit, yet I had the knowledge of his divine presence—we were heart to heart—and I received continuous strength.

For instance on Thanksgiving evening that week following the funeral, we attended a sacred concert, a previously arranged gift from dear friends. We would have preferred to withdraw, because we weren't in the mood for a concert. Yet we acquiesced to the constant encouragement from our friends and the promise that it would be "just what we needed," and attended the event as scheduled.

The music, though flawlessly rendered, was of a contemporary nature and that night in particular we were not responding to it. Just before the intermission, the guest star of the evening, Frank Boggs, stepped to the center of the stage. His rich baritone voice sang out so smoothly and meaningfully,

"Fill my cup Lord, I lift it up Lord,
Come and quench this thirsting of my soul."

That did it! We could identify with this song. We found ourselves being filled with a wonderful sense of God's love, caring, and understanding—a knowing he had not forgotten us, that he was right there, and everything was under complete control. In the stillness of our hearts' disarray, the tears flowed freely and we took comfort. We gave quiet thanks to our Heavenly Father. That was only the beginning of many such fillings, one after another, to keep us buoyed. We would not drown in our grief.

We have come a long way since then. God has been showing us how sorrow can be used constructively and triumphantly. We are better persons for having passed through the experience, and God knew it would be so—it always is, if we will let him accomplish it. If we are able to recognize God even in tragedy, then the suffering does not break us, it makes us. And trouble does have a permitted place. As J. Sidlow Baxter has said, "We can make all our circumstances contribute to the development of our Christian lives if we will. When in sorrow and trouble we often make our richest discovery of all that Christ can be to a human heart. The old oak log must be laid on the fire and the flames encircle it before its imprisoned music is set free. 2 Corinthians 4:17–18 says, 'For our light affliction which is but for a moment, worketh for us a far more weight of glory, while we look not at the things which are not seen; for the things which are seen are temporal, but the things which are not seen are eternal.' In the midst of seemingly interminable adversity, Paul would have us see the transient present against the everlasting glory which is yet to be."

I went to the car to get a few garden tools and the flowering plants I had purchased to place in the ground around Diane's grave. Digging into the soft earth in preparation, I wondered, "Why this urgency to be at her grave?" I wasn't sure. I do know God has a high regard for the human body; he created it in his likeness. Also, no one easily forgets the physical image of the ones loved so dearly. Could these be valid reasons?

I fully realized Diane's body was slowly turning to the dust of the earth. "Thou takest away their spirit, they die, and return to their dust" (Ps. 104:29b). I didn't dwell on that fact, however. My attention was given over to the precious truth that God had taken her spirit to be with him, alive and forever. "We are confident, I say, and willing rather to be absent from the body, and to be present with the Lord" (2 Cor. 5:8). I knew she was in Heaven, happy and safe. I also knew she would never return to me or to this earth in any other form. 2 Samuel 12:23 records David's statement at the death of his son, "He cannot come back to me, but I can go to him." He understood the biblical truth that his son was forever with God. I understood this regarding Diane also.

Then, too, the Scripture teaches there will come a moment when Diane's body will be brought forth from her grave a glorified and incorruptible body, to decay and die never again. It will be joined to her spirit in perfectness like that of Christ's resurrected body, for all the ages of eternity. 1 Thessalonians 4:16–18 is rich in comfort regarding this:

> For the Lord himself shall descend from heaven with a shout, with the voice of the archangel, and with the trump of God; and the dead in Christ shall rise first; then we who are alive and remain shall be caught up together with them in the clouds, to meet the Lord in the air; and so shall we ever be with the Lord. Wherefore, comfort one another with these words."

As time elapsed, I found myself thinking almost entirely of the good and happy experiences our family shared together. The grotesque details of Diane's death seldom came to the fore, as they used to. This day in my contemplative mood, I was capturing again some remarkably good times.

Diane had so many interests that changed so often, she kept us all amused. At one time she wanted to own a horse and enter races. She was learning to ride horseback and loved it, but she had some comical experiences and some close calls. I don't think she would ever have made racing—it was all she could do to just ride! At another time she was going to grow up to be a deep sea diver. She had a large collection of shells from various places and she was keenly interested in underwater life. Another time, she was going to be a conservationist because she enjoyed knowing about all kinds of trees, bushes, flowering things, and wild animal life. Then she was going to be a professional skier and become famous and rich. But she was better at falling than skiing! She did grow up to become a beautiful young girl, pursuing none of these interests. It is just that she loved life and everything connected with it.

I recalled the time our wedding anniversary fell on Mother's Day. The day before, our three children took Bob and me out to eat at a downtown restaurant in honor of the double celebration. There were corsages, boutonnieres, presents, and a merry time spent eating a superb meal in an appealing atmosphere. After dining, we were chauffeured (for that night, ours was the back seat) to where "The Greatest Story Ever Told" was being shown, extremely conscious that our children were doing this because they loved us, and experiencing a sense of healthy pride and gratitude.

I will not easily forget the impact the film had on our lives. We were caught up with what was happening and felt very much like participants. The crucifixion scene was so awesomely graphic that as we were leaving, Diane sobbed over and over, "He did all that for me! . . . He suffered so horribly for me! How awful it had to be when God turned away from him for one black moment—it was my sin that forced God to do it." It was quiet in the car except for her weeping. Then in kind of an emphatic whisper she said, "Oh, I love him so much for all of it!" Only God knows how thankful I was that Diane understood what God in Christ had accomplished on the cross for her.

A year later, May 22nd to be exact, we celebrated Diane's eighteenth birthday. She had chosen the dinner menu—a delicious high calorie one—a meal fit for a queen. What she didn't know was that we had invited a group of her church and school friends to be our guests. She hadn't suspected anything unusual for we always made our birthday dinners special.

While Diane was back and forth getting herself ready, her guests were silently sneaking in one by one to stand behind their chairs in the dining room. Suddenly Diane burst into the room with "How do I look, glam-er-?" Before she could finish her question, her friends in chorus shouted, "Surprise" and sang "Happy Birthday" to a startled, speechless, and then radiantly happy Diane. We ate with much talk and laughter, and afterwards the group played games and stood around the organ to do some singing before they broke up. I have always been glad for this time, because in a few weeks many of these friends, including Diane, graduated from high school and their paths took them in many different directions. This would be the last time they could ever meet again in this way.

At the grave I looked at my watch. The time had slipped

away. I turned again, and the freshly planted flowers were moving gently with the wind. I read once more:

DIANE RUTH BRISTOL

Born May 22, 1949—Died November 17, 1970

And I prayed, as I often do, "Dear Father, I do thank you that Diane is with you, safe from all the devastating goings-on here on earth. You were kinder than I can ever understand in taking her to yourself. Please remind her of how very much I love her. And, will you please give her a special hug for me? You know how deeply I miss her physical presence. Place your strong and gentle arms around her, for she is precious. I am glad you understand my heart in these matters. In Christ's name, Amen."

Nearly a year has passed since I took this journey. I may never take it again. The cemetery, as such, has much less attraction for me today. What my mother-heart seemed to need was met a year ago. I believe I am past that need now. When I think of Diane it is almost never with the vision of her body placed six feet in the earth. Instead I see, ever and always, a glimpse of her glowing happy face in the presence of her Savior, enjoying Heaven to its very fullest. She is in the very best of hands.

"For God who commanded the light to shine out of darkness, hath shined in our hearts, to give the light of the knowledge of the glory of God in the face of Jesus Christ." 2 Corinthians 4:6

15.
Valuable Lessons

As I wrote the words of the previous chapter, I found myself thinking of the many paths of the world Diane had walked, and of the endless encounters with new philosophies and ways of life! I would have spared her all of it had I been able. However she was learning some needed and valuable lessons, for after having pursued them all, she realized God's way is best. Dr. Cox's counsel, the day before she left for Hawaii, had proved true.

I too was learning some needed and valuable lessons: instruction in patience, in tolerance, in acceptance, in understanding. My need to continue learning in these areas is great. In addition, God is helping me to see that he has many and varied methods of working to accomplish beautiful results in people's lives, far more than our best minds can even begin to grasp. He simply is not limited to the ways in which we would have him work. He breaks through our plans and theories, and performs his perfect will—in his way.

I am learning about another side to prayer in which I have been inexperienced. God takes me seriously! I knew that, but I had not been allowing myself to be particularly conscious of it. Suddenly it was imperative that I really put thought into my prayer life. I have said many words without much thinking at all. My motives were always forthright and open, I rationalized. Actually I had never given them too much consideration, until the time Dr. Cox cautioned us as to motives. On close scrutiny, I found my motives to be thoughtless and altogether selfish many times. I had never known myself in this way and found it painfully revealing to have self-righteous attitudes surface like this.

It is amazing and a bit frightening when we honestly look at ourselves. I find I often hedge when I am forced to face my real self. The appalling part is to be unaware of "vain words" and "selfish motives." What a blow it was to my ego upon discovering dishonesty in my prayer life.

I am thankful, though, for this revelation. It is only when any problem is recognized that it can be dealt with. To be the honest person I desire, the Holy Spirit must keep these hidden places of my life uncovered. This has now become my prayer, for it is only as I see these trouble spots that they can be handled and resolved in any kind of satisfactory manner.

I am beginning to perceive there is not only darkness in spiritual unbelief, but also spiritual darkness in *belief*. It is easy to *say* I believe, but not to live like it. How essential it is not only to let God's Word be "a lamp unto my feet and a light unto my path," but also to walk in the light I have. Obedience, no matter how difficult the circumstances, ultimately produces beauty and fragrance in my life.

In the slowness of this process it is reassuring to know that I can come to God and bare my heart in complete undisguised honesty. He knows me so thoroughly anyway, and in my coming there is help for growth in these freshly uncovered areas of my life. Again God's word proves true: "Now we can come fearlessly right into God's Presence assured of his glad welcome when we come with Christ and trust in him" (Eph. 3:12, LB). "So let us come boldly to the very throne of God and stay there to receive His mercy and to find grace to help us in our times of need" (Heb. 4:16, LB).

I was honest with God that day back when mother, Dr. Cox and I prayed for Diane. My motives were above-board, I had given them inspection, and therefore could accept the fact that God had brought Diane to himself in his way. But it was not the kind of answer I was looking for, and my honesty brought pain that had to be lived with for days. My prayer was answered, however. God had done exactly what was asked of him along with a clear demonstration of how his ways are not my ways.

This experience has caused me to stop and think soberly and long now before making prayer requests. Do I sincerely want God to handle them in his way which may not be mine at all?

God acted swiftly. Many people wait for years and years for prayer answers, some die without ever seeing the answer to their prayers. I am tempted, at times, to believe this was one answer I could have gladly waited for much longer. Yet I know God's timing is right. From the time our request was placed in God's hands in May, to the time it was undeniably answered in November, was a period of six short months. It became an important phase in my Christian experience to have personally observed movement from heaven.

It made me realize in a deep and solemn way that God is alive and powerful. He is watching and listening, working and caring—answering our petitions as he sees best. I needed this kind of demonstration. I had watched some unusual prayer answers involving others; I needed something out of the ordinary for me. And it came.

There is the problem of self-guilt to be dealt with. Bob and I pretty much knew what to do with it, but it was a lesson we

had to face and handle. As I mentioned in Chapter 7, after
Diane had gone, we could recall areas where we had surely
failed her. Sometimes, in looking back, we could honestly say
we had meant well, we had done our best. In other ways we
knew we had not done the best we knew; we could have done
better. Then regret and guilt followed—a punishing of ourselves for things done in the past that cannot now be changed.
We both knew looking back in this way was unhealthy. To
carry a constant load of guilt around becomes a drag on one's
Christian life. So we brought our guilt before God just as we
had so many other areas of our lives. We left it with him and
asked for the ability to now forget. We knew self-harassment
was of no value.

The message from the Bible was our help again. The prophet
Micah promised, "Thou [God] wilt cast all their sins into the
depths of the sea." I'm sure he meant the deepest depths where
they could never again be found. Paul wrote to the Romans,
"Where sin abounded, grace did much more abound."

One of my favorite verses is Isaiah 43:25: "I, even I am he
that blotteth out thy transgressions for mine own sake, and
will not remember thy sins." He does this "for his own sake"
—not mine. I like that. He apparently does not care to bother
at all remembering some guilt of mine that he had already
blotted out—it isn't even there! If God is willing to forgive
my guilt, blot it from his memory forever, and never dangle
it in front of my mind's eye again, then why should I? It is
difficult to forget in the way he forgets, but I can be aware
that he has forgotten, and therefore I need not dwell on it one
second more! I learn my lessons slowly—but God is patient in
his teaching and I am learning. Therefore, I can face confi-
dently ahead again and live the open and honest life I so
desire. This is a beautiful experience—guilt gone, and an eager-
ness to look and move onward.

Diane's friend Jill carried a load of guilt for a long time.
She and Diane had gone to Hawaii together but it was a year
after Diane's death before we heard from her. She wrote to us

and said she had been afraid to make contact in fear we would be blaming her for Diane's death. If she had not persuaded Diane to go to Hawaii with her (we hadn't known until then that she had done the persuading), the whole course of her life would have been different and she would not have died in this way. I wrote to Jill immediately and assured her of our love and that in no way did we blame her for Diane's death—the thought had never even occurred to us.

Jill came to visit us one day when she returned home to Detroit. How relieved she was to experience first-hand that we held no resentment toward her. The load of guilt is heavy indeed, whether it is imagined or fact, and now she was freed from its burden. We were glad along with her.

Brad, too, carried a tremendous load of guilt. After we had received the information that Diane's murderer had been apprehended, tried and sentenced to life imprisonment, I wrote to Brad. I wondered if it had appeared in any of the San Diego papers, and whether or not he knew. His answer was a jolt to Bob and me. Among other things, he said, "Now you can be comparatively sure it wasn't Diane's *boyfriend* who murdered her." What a shocking statement! What a heavy load! We had no idea he might believe in any way that we, or anyone else, suspected him in Diane's death. We quickly wrote to assure him we had never thought him guilty in the slaying of our daughter. I've thought about that many times since. It must have been more than he could carry at times. I wish we had known sooner and could have helped ease that load for him. It is gone from his heart now and I am glad, as is he. His real guilt is one of unbelief, and only Jesus Christ can relieve him of that heavy burden. We pray each day that this will happen, for Brad is important to God and to us.

Another important lesson I am in the process of learning is to be concerned about the reality of my life. I believe many of us Christians are not really living. The Apostle Paul stated about his life, "I am crucified with Christ, nevertheless I live, yet not I, but Christ liveth in me." Why would I ever be apathetic and listless spiritually when Christ is living his life in me? Have I gone through the motions for so many years that I automatically keep right on with little thought of what I am really saying to the world out there? More than anything, I want to be a *real* person, detached completely from anything counterfeit. I am not surprised that young people have made the accusations they have. They are weary with our "acting" and want to see something demonstrated that comes through to them as real.

God has used my own children to help me here. I credit them for the fact that one day I stopped and began to honestly look at myself and the Christians I know. Listening to what they and many of their friends were saying, I had to ask, was there any truth in what they were accusing us of? My observation was that, to a great degree, their criticisms were valid. They were seeing a church filled with mechanical Christians, quite sincerely going through the motions—and they were being turned off. They had developed an aversion to our inconsistencies. Our archaic phrases and antiquated quotes we had clung to from our youth seemed to them anything but fresh and relevant—just the same old outdated thing! As I thought about it, I knew it wasn't outdated, for the Bible is basically current and in-tune with today. But, I believe we had unthinkingly allowed our Christian living to become stagnant. Though we were authentic members of the family of God, we had simply fallen into a groove and become monotonous and self-satisfied in our faith. The young people's accusations were well founded.

I was challenged by this to allow the Holy Spirit to stir me up, to move me out of the rut I was enjoying and to come alive again spiritually. Oh, there was life all right, but it had become anemic, and the charges made by the youth were the stimulus needed for me. I did not like being counted a fake. I asked

God to forgive me for becoming lethargic and to please open my heart and mind fresh to vibrant life and joy and blessing in Christ Jesus.

During this time I had to face the truth about my relationships with my children, my husband, and my friends, and be honest about where I had failed. For instance, I realized I had been guilty of wanting my children to reach the goals I had for them, and of resisting when they refused to conform to my plans. Perhaps all parents have this tendency. It certainly isn't wrong for us to want them to dress well, to be immaculate (in *our* youth, dressing well mattered very much). It isn't wrong that we like to present them to our friends as the handsome, well-groomed children we knew them to be just a few short years ago. It cannot be all wrong to wish them prosperous futures with great successes and accomplishments. We do take pride in showing off or telling of their talents and abilities. And why should we not be proud of our children? We are happy when we realize that as they have grown into adulthood they have become responsible citizens, making worthwhile contributions to society and to God.

This attitude, however, can be a selfish one. It satisfies us. We are thinking of us. I realized I was humiliated and hurt when Diane didn't measure up to the pattern of life I had planned for her. But the real question is, why should our children conform to the framework we have built for them? We are not considering their thinking at all, but rather our own feelings of pride, hurt and rejection. That now seems selfish to me. What matters very much to us doesn't trouble them at all. They have learned to evaluate each other on the basis of who the person is, not on what she wears or how long his hair may be. Appearances do not get in the way of their ability to see worth and value in one another. Some of us have great difficulty seeing anything good because we cannot see past the hairstyle.

I had to ask myself another question. Did the fact that the young people were finding flaws in us, and therefore, rationalizing all kinds of behavior (because "after all, you have failed us and so has the church") mean that I should take what I felt to be a less than Christian position? I had to mentally get this straight and settled. God has unchanging moral laws and the Bible allows no excuse for breaking them, and neither must I. Just because times were changing didn't automatically mean all changes were good. I must not compromise the Bible's principles. Yet at the same time I can demonstrate love and understanding and a faith flowing with life. This is what communicates, I am learning. I am helpless if I cannot relate.

I am thankful for the circumstances that forced me to review this area of my life, and to be enabled to take a clear yet loving Christian stand. I am grateful to my children and their friends—what a beautiful gift they are and have given to me. I am glad Diane was allowed to see a "change in mom" before she left us. I had "matured" she said. I still find I am stranded at times, but in taking time to think on these lessons again, I am freed to move on. Each day is a beautiful one, growing and learning with God.

I am trying to learn the value of stepping into the other person's shoes and viewing a situation through his or her eyes. Again, thanks to my children, I am finding this an important step forward. I don't do it very well, but it enables me to see more clearly why certain actions are taken, why circumstances can drive a person to make drastic moves. I can understand better why a particular path I think good is not followed and what looks like an inferior one pursued. I see why a special life philosophy has been adopted, even though I don't agree with it. I can see obstacles, many questions, reasonings to cause delays, doubts, detours regarding important issues in life. I can see hang-ups and hassles I could have totally discounted from my own point of view. It helps me understand just a little better why the other person thinks and acts in a specific way, even though it may be erroneous. I am helped when I understand; it keeps me from making false accusations, jumping to wrong conclusions, or being judgmental. I have plenty of practicing ahead of me here, a whole lifetime, but I like what happens when I make the effort.

I recall how grossly mistaken Eli was in his judgment of Hannah, from an outward appearance only. An agonizing mother was in the house of the Lord (1 Samuel 1) pouring out the hurts of her soul and the desires of her heart before her loving God. Eli, priest in the House of the Lord, saw only her lips move and hearing no sound judged her to be drunk! More and more I affirm that all judgment should be left with God, who alone sees the heart and knows the true motives behind one's actions. Hebrews 4:13 says, "Neither is there any creature that is not manifest is his sight, but all things are naked and opened unto him with whom we have to do." God will make absolutely right judgments. I don't have to.

Diane was a remarkably good example regarding the judgment issue. She exposed me occasionally by saying, "Mom, you don't really know that, so how can you judge?" Now and then I would trip her up with a similar situation, and it became a big thing with both of us. It matters such a great deal to me now, that I have made it a special point in my praying, asking God to help me really try to see as another sees, and to keep me from passing judgment. I lose ground so often, but I desire to develop this kind of attitude. God will do the judging anyway, and fairly. Why should I get into the act? "For the Lord is watching his children, listening to their prayers: but the Lord's face is hard against those who do evil" (1 Pet. 3:12, LB).

Another beautiful lesson emerging as a result of Diane's death is a willingness to share the tremendous "God-happenings" in my life. I had held back on this, believing that people in general need to know how the Bible can meet their needs— not the personal experiences of others. I still believe the Bible is of utmost importance in revealing our need and the answer to those needs. However, God has been dealing with me. I realize the writing of this book is the sharing of a very moving and personal experience. My hope is that God will use it to meet someone's need. Many times I have been challenged to deeper service and stronger faith through reading of other shared experiences.

I noticed one day, in reading the account of the demon-possessed man in Mark 5:1–19, that in his gratefulness to Jesus for the miracle in his life, he wanted to go with the Master. Jesus, however, said "No, go home to your friends and tell them the wonderful things God has done for you; and how merciful he has been." The formerly demon-possessed man did just that, and the *Living Bible* says the people were awestruck by his story. And so was I. The part about "go tell" I had missed all these years.

God has helped to unlock my thinking and has given me a liberty in sharing the wonderful and eternal things he has been accomplishing in my life. In fact, the sharing aspect invariably opens the door for the gospel.

I am also learning more about sorrow and despair. They certainly do touch each one at some time in life and in varied ways. I am becoming aware that every single minute someone, somewhere, is suddenly broken down with the kind of grief and heartache I know about. It is very easy to go on from day to day just not thinking about the anguish in another's life which is intensely real and present. I can't possibly know all about everyone, nor is there any way, humanly, to stretch myself to help meet everyone's needs. But it is no problem for our God, and these people now have my prayers.

Along with the lessons being learned regarding despair and sorrow, I am learning more about the victory provided for my Christian life. God brought me from the darkness of despair and sorrow to victory—I *have* experienced this. It takes time, a lot of it, to push ahead in the long dark tunnel, but the light finally emerges through the darkness. And with it—victory. "If God be for us, who can be against us?" is the biblical word (Rom. 8:31), and he had been walking the dark lonesome valley too, closely and intimately, all those difficult months. This victory now makes life doubly worth living, and death—well—"to be absent from the body [is] to be present with the Lord" (2 Cor. 5:8). The Apostle Paul said that, and also this: "To be with Christ . . . is far better." To me this means victory for sure.

Diane's life was a demonstration to me of the importance of showing genuine love. Her death has made me see how necessary it is to show it *now,* because I may not get another chance. God has not only put his love in my heart, but he has gone before me and paved the way with his own perfect love, unlike that of any human being, so that I can point to him and be able to say with all confidence, "God loves you."

*"Arise, shine: for thy Light is come, and
the glory of the Lord is risen upon thee."*
Isaiah 60:1

16.
Thy Light Has Come

The time period in this last chapter is only one month after
Diane's death. I have purposely saved these incidents to share
in the closing chapter, because I believe they show how beauti-
fully God was bringing our lives from darkness into his glorious
light, even in those first weeks. "The people that walked in
darkness have seen a great light: they that dwell in the land
of the shadow of death, upon them hath the light shined"
(Isa. 9:2).

In the days following Diane's death, we began the rush toward Christmas, which I found to be a direct blessing from
God. The extensive involvement with this season was a kind
of therapy I needed. I allowed myself to become completely
absorbed with Christmas preparations in my determination
not to be swallowed up by death, but rather with *Life*. We
were soon to celebrate the birth of the One whose very purpose
was to bring life to man. "In him was life; and the life was the
light of men" (John 1:4). I intended this Christmas to be the
greatest and most meaningful of all.

One of Diane's friends had written, "I am sure we are all
glad that Diane is enjoying the best Christmas ever because she

is spending his birthday with him and she is *free* at last." I knew this was true, yet with her death not far behind us, I found my humanness desperately reaching for her at times.

She had left her Christmas list with us before she returned to California: Food blender

New English Bible with the Apocrypha

Money toward stereo components

Guitar

Teflon egg poacher

Etc.

It was not going to be easy facing this season without her physical presence.

Then I thought of the message that had come from my cousin at the time of Diane's passing:

> May the Christ of Christmas be especially real and near to you this year. The joy and peace that comes from our relationship with Him shines more brightly in the darkness, and e-x-p-a-n-d-s to fill the emptiness when other joys fade. When I lost my brother just before Christmas a few years back, I thought there could be no Christmas—and then I discovered that I had never really known what it meant before—and Christmas has never been the same since.

"Oh, Christ of Christmas," I prayed, "please show me how to keep my heart open so that all the glory of God may shine through. Fill the emptiness with the radiant reality of your shining presence as only you, dear Christ, can do."

David had made plans to spend Christmas in New York State. This meant that our family would celebrate Christmas one week early. So, for the first time since we had established a family, Bob and I found ourselves spending the real Christmas Eve (normally a gala family occasion) entirely alone. I was acutely aware of the situation, and knew we dared not just sit and think, something must be planned. I was aware, also, that Bob was thinking the same.

I made the suggestion that we have our regular Christmas Eve dinner with candles, music and tree lights, as usual, and Bob agreed. The fact we had celebrated a week earlier didn't mean much now. Bob selected some Christmas music to be playing softly as we dined.

Bob offered a prayer to God and, with broken voice, prayed something like this: "Our Father, first of all, we thank you for your Son, the Lord Jesus Christ. If you had not sent him to this earth, we would still be in our sin. We thank you for this 'unspeakable gift' of love given us on the first Christmas night so long ago. We thank you, Father, for standing so close to us when we needed you more than at any other time in our lives. You have supplied us continually with the much needed grace and strength in a beautiful way. You have not failed us and have held us together. We pray again, O God, for the healing that is so necessary for our anguished hearts. We thank you for your provision of food this Christmas Eve. In Christ's name, Amen."

As we lifted moist eyes, it seemed to me I could envision some of the shining radiance and glow for which I had prayed.

After we had eaten and I had put the dining room and kitchen back in order, Bob drew me into the living room. He had positioned two lounge chairs, "so we can enjoy the full effect of stereo sound," he stated.

The tree lights were glimmering through the tinsel and trimmings. The softly flickering candles sent shadows and sweet aroma throughout the room. The atmosphere was lovely. Bob pushed the turntable controls and from the stereo speakers came forth the magnificent sounds of Handel's *Messiah*.

> Comfort ye, comfort ye my people,
> saith your God . . .

Ah, yes, this was what we needed tonight, and the tears began falling unashamedly down our faces.

The people that walked in darkness have seen a great light:
they that dwell in the land of the shadow of death,
upon them hath the light shined."

And the glory, the glory of the Lord
shall be re - veal - ed.

And on through all the lovely solos and chorus selections.
Then finally, in all of its glory and power and triumph—

> Hallelujah!
> For the Lord God Omnipotent reigneth.
> King of kings and Lord of lords
> King of kings and Lord of lords
> Hallelujah! Hallelujah!
> Hallelujah! Hallelujah!
> *Hal - le - lu - jah!*

And the light of Christ's presence expanded and filled the
emptiness and, for us, Christmas can never be the same again!
Life can never be the same again! Christ's presence has made
our sorrow *something beautiful.*